EMPTY NEST, FULL OF LIFE

7 Secrets & 16 Lessons to:
Overcome Empty Nest Syndrome,
Refocus on Yourself, and Live a Fulfilled Life

Birguy Lamizana Diallo

WHAT OTHERS ARE SAYING . . .

"I . . . have three grown children. Reading Empty Nest made me not only remember but also reflect on how little attention I gave to this very important matter when my children started leaving the nest. I just assumed that life needs to continue and did not address what I needed to do to soothe or to enhance my feelings when the children started leaving. I am not surprised with the beautiful crafting of this book by Birguy.

Since I met her on a marvelous trip in Pretoria, South Africa in 2018, I was attracted by her kindness and her ability to bring people together. I found myself attracted to her and to our deep conversations about life, business and parenting. In those conversations, Birguy was always warm, reflective and inspirational. We kept in touch because every time we had the opportunity to talk there was growth in me. We then coincidently found ourselves in the same training in Croatia. We had the opportunity to share a holiday apartment; just the two of us and again our conversations were like two sisters reuniting after a long period away from one another. We had fun, we learned a lot from one another, and we shared resources.

That is how I got to meet Keith, Birguy's son, who helped me with the illustration for my own book. In my first meeting with Keith, I could hear Birguy in our conversation, I could see and feel how structured as a person and professional Keith was and that confirmed my own understanding of how Birguy as an educator and a mentor to her children as influenced the way Keith presented himself.

His level of clarity, persistence, elegance and the delicate manner that he went about his business was definitely influenced by his mum. The beautiful work Keith did, and that I am proud of, has to do with his talent, however the way he presents it, is a reflection of the beautiful, strong and caring foundation that he found in the nest.

I have learned so much from this humble daughter of the divine. I can proudly say that Humanity grows and progresses with personalities like Birguy because they always see and build a better world, with no judgments, where there is room for all and space for individuals to live their own identity with dignity. Giving my testimony is a great opportunity for me to say thank you to Birguy for inspiring us to greatness."

-Helena Zefanias Lowe, writer and adult educator, Mozambique

"I have known Dr. Birguy Lamizana [professionally] for several years. Her outstanding accomplishments have been acknowledged internationally and inspires many by her approach that ensures developing multi-stakeholder engagement and intergenerational partnerships in solving the environmental problems especially conservation and management of natural resources. Apart from being a professional of international stature playing a key role in reducing land degradation, she is an excellent inspiring human-being at large. I recall some of our discussions in the last more than seven years where she has inspired me and many like me to have work-life balance, a key for many women in professional space.

Her dedication for leading a healthy lifestyle where there is a place for her family, her children, her health, her hobbies, traveling and much more makes her very different from many professionals who keep complaining about less time and being very busy to find time for meaningful things. I was awestruck to know how she manages time by finding time for many important things in those precious 24 hours that we all have.

Her book on "Empty Nest" is an interesting and thought provoking read that I am sure will help many mid-career parents to start planning that stage of life a little earlier than otherwise in a better way. I really admire her approach of penning down her experiences from an empty nest to be shared with the world for larger benefits of society. I wish her the best with her new role as an author and am sure she will excel in that, too."

—Shalini Dhyani, Senior Scientist CSIR NEERI India

"I had the pleasure of traveling with Birguy to wonderful places, and, although we were there for intense working sessions, we always found the way to

explore where the meeting was taking place.
In those short moments when we could walk around, feel the crisp Himalayan mountain air, the astonishing beaches of Mozambique, or the freezing waters of the Baltic Sea in our feet, Birguy always had warm and mothering advice for me.
For instance, she encouraged me to finish my PhD as a single mom, telling me the process of her experience of doing a PhD as mother of three while working full-time. Reading the book feels like talking with Birguy with her affection and wisdom. I will cherish her words in the times ahead."
—Manuela Ruiz Reyes, 41, single mother of a teenager, ecologist-geographer, Colombia

“Birguy is a proud family woman who lives for her children. Like me, she wants what’s best for her children and tries to set an example without doing everything for them. This book is a good example of her efforts to assist without doing things directly for her children. Birguy is a consummate professional, and I know her best in that role. As such, her foray into the literary world was quite a pleasant surprise, and I’m happy to see this piece of work, which should help others relate to her experience as a mature mother.”
—Vincent Sweeney, Head, Caribbean Sub-Regional Office, UNEP, Kingston, Jamaica

"I have known Birguy Lamizana since 2013 when she invited me to join the Global Wastewater Initiative under her leadership at the United Nations Environment Programme. Birguy is a remarkable leader believing in team building and collaboration, a colleague with immense talent and skills, and a fine human being. I share so many thoughts expressed by Birguy Lamizana in her book, which would undoubtedly help readers transition to an empty nest.
—Manzoor Qadir, Ph.D, Deputy Director, UNU-INWEH, Hamilton, Canada

"Birguy has written about an issue that concerns every parent sooner or later: the empty nest syndrome: how we feel, when the nest is empty, and what we can do about it when we feel bad about our empty nest. Birguy has given us some guidance and wisdom derived from her own life's experiences. In writing a very mindful book for all parents who feel the pang of an empty nest when the children are gone, Birguy has also let us take a glimpse into her life and career. She showed us how a little Fulani girl from a small village in West Africa reached to the stars and made her far-fetched dream come true. The book is an inspiration to all those who have fulfilled their parenting role and must seek new sense and meaning in life. But it is perhaps an even greater inspiration to those who have a big dream. For they will learn from this book that you can realize your dream, however big, with dedication and determination and the mutual love and support of a family. Enjoy the read!

—Gisela Mahler, Saarbrücken, Germany

Birguy. Our friendship started from a drop, like water, and it kept running, like water, for several years. And I am sure it will continue. Because water is life.

Birguy. A strong, courageous, and determined women who learned how to make things happen the way she decided. She likes to discover, to laugh, to relax, to enjoy life, but most importantly she is dedicated, she works hard, ... and knows how to make the difference, for others and for herself.

There is nothing more inspiring than reading about the experiences of persons we cherish, because their words are nothing but precious and their feelings are so genuine. This book is so profound; I thought it speaks to me at a certain time, I relate in some situations. I discovered different sides of your life that we did not had time to share. Your book has answered questions I have never had the opportunity to ask you: How have you made it during these long years while being a mom and a wife living far from your beloved, traveling so often and fulfilling hard tasks? Now I understand what you have been through.

We have been sharing memorable moments in various continents and cities: Perou, Dresden, Dar-saalam, Addis, Stockholm, Tunis, etc. We worked together and we laughed together. I'm grateful for the wonderful moments we shared and the opportunities you offered me to be part of your network and circle of friends. I enjoyed working with you and appreciated your diligence and team spirit.

I should recognize that your book has come at a very critical moment of my life, may be a turning point, where several of the questions you have been raising are spinning in my head. One thing you can be sure of is that your book will be one of my best readings and I look forward to receiving the hard copy to dive into it from time to time. Birguy, you are a special woman. Thank you for being you and for sharing pieces of your life. Glad to be part of your venture.

— Olfa Mahjoub, your friend from Tunisia

"Dr. Birguy Lamizana and I met in our Best Seller in Action group where I had an instant connection because she is so supportive and encouraging. Her book is a transformational book on the empty nest syndrome and the secrets she shares are bound to help you navigate this phase of life. She openly shares her personal experiences which are so vast and relatable. Congratulations on writing this book.

—Dr Ukpong Nwankwo, London, UK

"It was in the early nineties and I was in Ouagadougou for the wetlands management programme of IUCN, the International Union for the Conservation of

Nature. I was briefed by a young programme officer, who introduced herself as Birguy Lamizana. She was warm and friendly, but also to the point and very correct towards this mustached consultant from The Netherlands. The appreciation was mutual. It remained until this day.

Over the years we met and worked occasionally together. Birguy was very much a family-person and she missed husband and children. How she managed, far away from home and as the warm and attractive person that she is. We both missed our families while abroad and talking about our partners and children helped, but still.... I am, like so many of us, an expert in what Birguy describes as the empty nest syndrome.

- Empty nest? What empty nest, Birguy?

Wherever Birguy goes she radiates warm cordiality, she extends her family, people become part of her not-so-empty nest. At the same time she cherishes the family-ties with her own "siblings". How? It is all in this wonderful book. I read it and I know Birguy now even better. It is rich in lessons that make you think about your own past and present situation, and how to enjoy a full life in future. Lesson ONE for me: There may be a syndrome, but there is no empty nest! We all are family. Dear Birguy, thank you!

—Piet Wit, The Netherlands

"I was privileged to meet Dr. Birguy Lamizana early in her distinguished career as an expert in Integrated Water Resource Management. Birguy came to the United States in 2003 as a participant in the International Visitor Leadership Program (IVLP), an elite program of the U.S. Department of State's Bureau of Educational and Cultural Affairs. Established after WWII to foster positive relations between the countries of the world, the IVLP has brought hundreds of thousands of up-and-coming leaders from across the globe, hundreds of whom have ultimately into positions of leadership within their countries. Birguy Lamizana was one of those up-and-coming leaders back in 2003 on an environmental project. At that time, she had distinguished herself through her work with the IUCN, the International Union for the Conservation of Nature, where she coordinated the wetlands and water program for West Africa. Since that time, she has created a strong record of accomplishments in developing actions plans in IWRM for West and Eastern Africa's countries and coordinating partnerships. As evidenced in her latest endeavor, an exploration of the Empty Nest Syndrome, Birguy has, throughout her intensive career, also experienced the joys of motherhood – along with its vicissitudes, particularly when the children leave their familial nest. Recognizing the global nature of this syndrome,

Birguy provides some comparative analysis of empty nest syndrome in differing cultures. I have never been a mother, but I watched my own mother as she struggled to adjust to the empty nest. One of her coping mechanisms was to write a poem to each of us as we prepared to leave. The one to me still makes me cry. Birguy knows of what she speaks. I hope you will read and gain insights from this new book.
—Joanne Clark, Senior Program Officer (ret.), Meridian International Center, Washington, DC, USA

I had the pleasure of meeting Birguy for the first time in 2018. Not only did I meet her, but I joined her team to work on addressing the challenges of wastewater management on the global level with the United Nations Environment Programme (UNEP) in Nairobi, Kenya. Besides having been an excellent supervisor, Birguy has also been a mentor and family to me. Many of the achievements and opportunities I had in the past few years are also thanks to the role she had and continues to have in my life, as well as her guidance and support.
Birguy's book is not only a practical guide on addressing change after children leave their nest, but more in general, it is a guide for everyone when going through changes and challenges in life. It is practical yet filled with care, love, and teachings from her life experiences. It is a book that inspires every reader to become a better version of her or himself and that, as

she puts, “encourages you to dream bigger, believe in yourself and enjoy your journey to greatness.” Birguy had such a positive influence and role in my life. As she continues to inspire me, I am sure she will do the same with you through this wonderful book.
—Riccardo Zennero, Nairobi, Kenya

'Having built businesses in the travel space with Birguy and enjoying the fruits of our travel and personal development lifestyle I can say she has a complete grasp of reality and approached life in a methodical and planned way - so she always made sure life was lived to its highest capacity. Additionally, we also worked in the global skincare and healthcare sector where she showed her versatility and ability to juggle all of life’s facets seamlessly - but mostly, again, learning the deep connection that it takes to make anything worthwhile last as we built teams and team spirit while enjoying the industry we were in.
I know this book is a culmination of much thought and life experience and can be a handbook to anyone who simply takes their time to apply her knowledge which is coming from a place of love.Know that Birguy is a formidable woman who knows what she wants and has the inspiration and internal fortitude to go after it.’
—Anand Patel, Zimbabwe & USA

My friend, Author Birguy Lamizana
The biggest change for me as an empty nester mom was realizing I needed to put someone else before me. Now the hardest part about the empty nest is learning to put yourself first. As the lessons from parents and children have clearly stated, parents can only give good advice or put them on the right paths. After dealing with this syndrome, I come to realize your life can be even better in many ways because you now have more time and other resources available to you, So I cheer you on with your dreams and dare you to live it. This book is worth the read, especially when you can finally create a life that supports your own needs and desires. I recommend this book to anyone experiencing an empty nest.
—Christine James, Author, USA

"Practical down to earth advice, tableted in the form of a great book, for those who make up the majority of the population, in any country, for when we are separated from our roots as a result of entering the next era of our lives. I have known Birguy for several years now. She has become a close friend and business partner. Together we have traveled much, cried, laughed and simply enjoyed each other's company. I will always admire her tenacity, great energy and steadfastness for pursuing her dreams and goals. What a privilege to be in her life."
—Sandy Lowe, business woman (Harare, Zimbabwe)

“’Birguy comes up with an easy-to-practice, a top-notch book which rightly retraces the trajectory of every individual during his whole life. Being in an endless pilgrimage on this earth, we are doomed to move from one place to another, leaving loving people behind and coming across new ones. This move brings in new challenges and changes which require adjustments and call for coping mechanisms to adapt. For this, the book provides hands-on recipe, each colored page we turn after another bringing in new ingredients.

Beyond the author’s autobiographic information, this inspirational book is a pathway to live a full, meaningful, and purposeful life which doesn’t happen overnight. The author puts the finger on what constitutes the matter of concerns for conservative parents (like me) who never think to let children leave the nest one day. With the practical instant actions in hands and through the experience sharing, resourceful materials provided and inspiring secrets as clues, this book helps get prepared for the unavoidable empty nest syndrome.

On the other hand, having the same trajectory in my lifetime across a series of nests, starting from my village to the big cities in my home country then to Burkina Faso thanks to education opportunity, I am one of the appropriate persons to provide testimony since this perpetual move continues till now for career obligations.

Back to the author per se, I am one of the twelve classmates who was closer to her, and maybe also the one who shared the most with her. As such, I am supposed to know a little bit of her. In fact, our road crossed in 1987 when we entered the university of Ouagadougou to study in the field of Geology. This will last 5 more memorable years of togetherness, friendship, familiarity and a high sense of belonging to a united and compact team of twelve students called CEE in reference to the European Economic Commission at the time.
I would like to highlight just 2 major facts to support my proximity with Birguy:

- School holiday 1988: always loving to travel, Birguy had to go to Freetown, Sierra Leone, with her friends. She entrusted me with her Econo Power motorcycle, one of the few on campus at the time, while the large majority of students were riding mobylettes. The motorcycle was in my care for the whole summer. What a sign of confidence! Birguy being a well-known girl in the city, everyone noticed her bike and asked me questions about her whereabouts.

- Hydrogeology data collection: we were in 1992, in our 5th year of the engineering cycle. Professor SAWADOGO Nindawa (RIP), who was teaching us hydrogeology, wanted to initiate us to research in a practical way. The 12 students were divided into pairs to go into the field. Naturally, it was not difficult for me to find my pair for the terrain. Aboard a CROSS motorcycle provided by the school, Birguy and I had to go to Kongoussi and Djibo to collect data from ONEA (National Water & Sanitation Office). We took turns driving the big motorcycle and Birguy once again showed her abilities as a girl very capable of doing exactly what men can do. I must point out by the way that of the 12 students, there were only 2 girls. Geology was not a field of attraction for girls certainly because of the roughness of the curriculum and the demands of field trips. Indeed, we would have to be constantly in the field during our entire formation, climbing mountains and other rocky escarpments, some culminating over 1000 m. There too, Birguy and her girlfriend did not fail the challenge. Moreover, there was no gender bias in our class and this perception is jealously preserved to now, all of us being brothers and sisters.

Even back to my country, I have maintained regular contacts so far with some of my graduates, particularly Birguy, with whom we often meet at international meetings, such as in Dakar, Senegal in 2006 and in Cape Town, South Africa in February 2019. At this latter meeting we realized that 3 of our classmates passed away. As usual, Birguy immediately had the idea to create a WhatsApp group chat of the promotion upon her return to Nairobi where she was based at the time. This has been done since then and our CEE WhatsApp platform could reconnect the 9 of us, still alive, thanks to Birguy's initiative. Regardless of our social status, we regularly spend time exchanging, joking, and teasing each other like little children. We really enjoy it and have fun. Even though most of us are senior officials in the administration of our respective countries and international civil servants, this platform makes us maintain our student spirit. It is a real melting pot of unity, fraternity and solidarity. And on behalf of the CEE group I say a big thanks to Birguy for this wonderful initiative.

—Hoba Rogoto, Birguy's class mate, CEE"

PUBLISHED BY: Birguy Lamizana Diallo, Inc.

Paperback ISBN: 978-3-9825756-0-5

Cover art: Kolene Laury Lamizana
Layout:
Book illustration: Kolene Laury Lamizana

Published by:
Birguy Lamizana Diallo, Inc.
Bonn, Germany
www.emptynestfulloflife.com

DEDICATION

With respect, admiration and sincere appreciation, I dedicate this book to my wonderful family. Without you and the lessons you have taught me throughout my life, I would not have the blessing of being where I am today. Thank you from the bottom of my heart! I love you dearly!

MOTIVATE AND INSPIRE OTHERS!
“SHARE THIS BOOK

Click [Here]For Order...

TABLE OF CONTENTS

A MESSAGE FOR YOU

You may be wondering: what is the empty nest syndrome? And why is someone writing about it?
The truth is, children leaving home for university, marriage, or a new job causes a significant adjustment for many parents that often results in feelings of loss, grief, and loneliness. This phenomenon is known as the empty nest syndrome.

Raup and Myers[1] define the empty nest syndrome as a poor response of parents transitioning to a lifestyle where their children are no longer center. This poor response is understandable as, unlike the young of lesser animals, human young take years of intense upbringing before becoming independent, a time that consolidates the ties and habits of togetherness.

Despite technological advances that bridge communication gaps, the empty nest syndrome has been a reality for generations as parents continue to experience that familiar sense of loss, grief, and anxiety once their children leave the nest. Don't get me wrong; the symptoms aren't always negative. Relief and excitement about a new life chapter can also be

[1] Raup, J. & Myers, J. E. (1989). The empty nest syndrome: Myth or reality? Journal of Counseling and Development, 68(2) 180-183.

part of the empty nest experience for parents and children.

In many African and Asian cultures, traditional family structures include extended family or several generations living under the same roof, which lessens the emotions from the empty nest.
To have children move to live with relatives is also common, in contrast with modern families who tend to follow the nuclear family structure most often found in Europe or America. When children leave, in this nuclear family context, parents tend to suffer from empty nest syndrome. Regardless of cultural or geographical differences, leaving the parental nest at some point is inevitable and is often affected by factors, such as labor, market conditions, level of financial independence/dependence, educational opportunities, marriage, the affordability of housing, and cultural distinctiveness.

Leaving the parental nest for educational opportunities is a natural next step in life since formal education is typically divided into four stages: early childhood, primary, secondary, and tertiary. For example, in most developing countries, the lack of public resources in education may require children to leave the parental nest earlier, whether they are sent from rural areas to the city or from one city to another within the country or abroad. In contrast, when conditions are favorable and opportunities present, children may leave the parental nest at a later stage (for employment or when entering a relationship with a partner), as is often the case in Western countries. Also true in some cases, particularly in Europe or America, is that children are responsible after high school to pursue their education or other goal. Many have to make that choice and find funding themselves, which often necessitates a loan to get them started. In any case, the later children leave the parental nest, the better emotionally prepared the parents are to handle their departure.

Another situation with which parents deal is the return of grown children after they have been on their own for a time. Indeed, once the child leaves, parents adjust and reinvent a new way of living. Unfortunately, adult children's inability to maintain financial independence increasingly leads them to move back in with parents, thus refilling the empty nest. The return of the fledgling adult is not always easy for parents or children. Once parents have invested in new roles to replace parental responsibilities, their adult children's financial and emotional dependence can be burdensome.

You must be wondering: how does this empty nest syndrome apply to Birguy Lamizana?

In fact, our nest was emptied long ago.
Since then, my husband & I have been living alone in different countries. Friends and colleagues are used to seeing me live alone. Hence, when I speak at conferences, facilitate training courses, converse with colleagues, or just hang out with friends and interact with people, I am always asked the same questions: "How do you cope with living alone? Aren't you lonely? How do you manage?"

My answer to these recurrent questions is always the same: "In life, you have to learn to enjoy your own company. Once you do that, the company of others becomes a bonus." Of course, this did not happen with a snap of the fingers. Because I kept on getting this same question, over and over again, I reflected on how I was coping. Hence, I wrote this book to share my secrets, which are based on my experience and those of other parents and children who underwent a similar journey that included the changes that occurred, the adjustment we made, and the mechanisms we used to bounce back.

In one course I attended on resilience building, trainers defined resilience as: "bouncing back, bending but not breaking" and a trait that was able to be cultivated. Through this training and many others I have taken, I have learned and practiced life-changing strategies. I hope this book will be a gift to you that will make a positive difference in your life.

My goal with Empty Nest, Full of Life is to inspire and motivate you to transform difficult situations into opportunities for growth and to find what gives your life meaning, purpose and fulfillment. I want to share my insights and the insights of other parents and children who flew the nest. I want to share golden tips and secrets that helped me. I hope these inside pointers will prepare you to recognize and cope with an empty nest and grab the opportunity the available time offers as you refocus on yourself and the rest of your life.

Included are seven simple yet powerful secrets /strategies to embrace as you aim for a blissful life. The seven do not have to be read in order; flip through and find ones that speak to you. You will also find accounts from parents and children whom I have interviewed, each of whom experienced a different journey to which you can relate and learn. In addition, various resources are provided if you choose to deepen your knowledge and take the wheel of your own life.

Some secrets will be new; others will be familiar. Some will be easy to implement; others will require more effort. Some strategies will comfort you; others will require you to shift your paradigm and move out of your comfort zone. One thing is certain: these secrets will push you to think and act differently.

To meet you through this book is my honor and privilege—and I hope one day to meet you in person! Thank you for reading. When you finish, please share Empty Nest, Full of Life with friends and family to help them in their lives.

As James Malinchak rightly says: “The greatest gift you can ever receive is knowing you have made a difference in the lives of others.”

Birguy
Bonn, Germany
2023

HOW DO YOU HANDLE THIS CHANGE FOR A PURPOSEFUL LIFE?

"The quicker you let go of old cheese, the sooner you find new cheese."
_Dr. Spencer Johnson, Who Moved My Cheese?

The great lesson one can draw from Dr. Spencer Johnson's Who Moved My Cheese is:
things constantly change. The essence of physical existence is change. From a worm to an insect to a bird to a dumb animal to a tree—every one of them is trying to live a full-fledged life.

This is true for humans, too. At some point in time, everything we know changes for good or bad. Life habits change when we welcome children and help them grow into responsible adults, and again when they leave to be on their own.

Although normal in life, change can be difficult. To weather change successfully requires courage and discipline. If you resist change, you resist the whole process of life, and you will create unnecessary suffering.
Depression may become an ongoing struggle. As you age, change can become more difficult due to the comfort zones that buffer your life. Any disturbance to these cocoons of comfort may create a lack of balance in your life.

Everything is in flux; nothing is permanent. Of course, lots can happen that will transform who you are and have an impact on your life. Hence, cultivating the ability to accept whatever comes and embrace it is necessary. Although easier said than done, you must adapt. Albert Einstein said: “In the middle of every difficulty lies an opportunity.” Change does not necessarily mean crisis if you have the means to alter your experience of change.

Perhaps the psychological effect of being the one making the choice has a different impact from leaving the choice to the children. A deep reflection on what happened and how you feel about it is a starting point:

Was I choosing to see my children leave when I first chose their schools?
Would I choose differently?
How do I feel about my children navigating the world alone?
Do I worry about their being ready and well-equipped with the correct life tools?
Am I confident I prepared them enough?
Did I feel they were capable of safely navigating the world?
Did they ask for advice/help when needed?

Answering these difficult but necessary questions will help you assess your stance in terms of your feelings and emotions and of utmost importance, will help you see change as opportunity.

Next, ask yourself what might lie ahead for you now that your children have left the nest. Write down what is important to you—YOUR priorities—not the ones you think the world expects of you. My priorities are spending time in nature, traveling, listening to music, reading, and learning new skills. Some prioritize spending quality time with friends, or even waking up late now that they no longer have children to care for. Search for those positive aspects that make your life happier, fuller, and more meaningful, and focus on them. Ultimately, living purposefully means giving yourself time and space to do what makes you happy.

Renowned bestselling author Paulo Coelho said: "When we love, we always strive to become better than we are. When we strive to become better than we are, everything around us becomes better, too."

In the early years of my marriage, I was controlling and jealous. I lost my temper easily. I was not proud of that behaviour and reflected on how miserable I was focusing on my husband, trying to control him, and losing my temper with my children. I decided to focus on myself and sought an online course to learn how to let go of anger and jealousy and how to put myself first. Changing my thinking changed my life. I fell in love with who I am and began working toward a better version of myself.

Why am I telling you this? I want to show you from my experience that once you acknowledge a problem and address its root, change is possible. However: Don't try to fix other people. Fix yourself. This process helped me deal with an empty nest and pursue a journey of purposefulness.

Don't be afraid to ask yourself difficult questions, as the answers will illuminate your pursuits in life based on your own paradigm, your perspective, and the direction of travel you choose to take. Well known author Stephen R. Covey[2] (The 7 Habits of Highly Effective People) defines paradigms as maps of our perception or understanding of the world, maps that shape our attitudes and behaviors. Paradigms are powerful because they create the lens through which we see the world and thus determine the choices we make in life. Your perspective and paradigm affect the choice you make. Your perspective is the way you think and understand something. Your paradigm is the context inside your mind from which you think, feel, live, and it determines what you hold onto, mentally and emotionally. Your paradigm includes the way you conduct yourself, the way you interact with people, the way you build and nurture your family, raise your children, and hold onto them or let them go. As you can see, understanding the importance of what drives your decision-making process—your paradigm is crucial, particularly when dealing with change. This understanding is the first step toward handling the changes brought by the empty nest.

---

[2] Covey, Stephen R. The 7 Habits of Highly Effective People: 25th Anniversary Edition. New York: Simon & Schuster, 2004

When much of your life has been defined as a parent, finding it difficult to adjust to a life without your children is normal. You might feel lonely, especially in a big house with several empty bedrooms, and experience a deep void in your life.

However, of equal importance is deciding on the direction you want your journey to take and on the strategy you will use to bounce back should you run into difficulties. A small step like thinking of all the free time you now have and how to use it in a meaningful way could make a big difference in how you proceed. Hence, having more time is an opportunity, but if you are not mindful, your time will "disappear" into easy or low-value activities, e.g., addictive use of social media.

A switch I learned in a personal development course is one you can switch on whenever you find yourself in such a situation: think about RAIN. Accept being rained on, knowing that sunshine—and perhaps a rainbow—will follow.

- *Recognize what is happening.*
- *Allow the experience.*
- *Investigate with kindness.*
- *Nurture naturally.*

So let's embrace the RAIN!

INSTANT ACTION STEP

Take five minutes to think about and record the change that's happening in your life:

How are you handling this change?

____

____

____

What is your purpose in life?

____

____

____

How can you embrace RAIN?

____

____

____

How can you instill the ways of being into your life starting today?

____

____

____

SECRET #1

ACKNOWLEDGE WHAT IS HAPPENING; TAKE TIME TO THINK IT THROUGH AND, MAKE A GOOD DECISION.

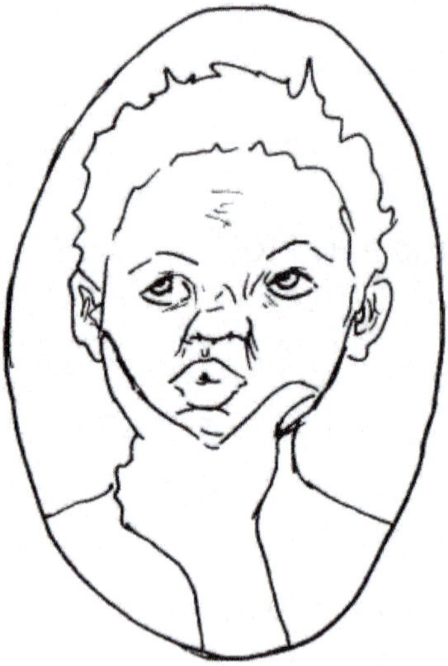

"Learning to acknowledge our negative emotions can be quite a scary prospect."
_Janine Fair

I wanted to have it all: get married, have children, and build a great career. A kind of balanced life, you would say. Illusion! Life is never balanced. I am grateful that I got marriage, children, and a career, but they did come with sacrifices.

There is always a trade-off in life. This willingness to have it all, was the driving force behind every decision I made in my life. As a matter of fact, the importance I placed on education played a significant role in my decision-making process. My relationship and feeling toward education are special; no matter what I have to go through, I will choose education first.

I wouldn't be the person I am today without the decisions I took at a very early age. At the age of six, I decided to leave my parents & follow my grandmother who lived in the city to be able to go to school. I wonder today how my parents felt back then. My dream was to go to school and fly in a plane. When playing with my agemates in the village, I would tell them:

"I am not going to be a shepherd, or to stay here and pound the millet or milk the cows.

I will go to school and fly in these airplanes you are seeing above us, high in the sky!"

My dream came true when my grandmother, Coumbo Barkey ([1929-1998] may she continue to rest in peace), visited, and I convinced her to take me with her and enroll me in school.

Let me pause here to tell you a bit about this amazing woman. Indeed, my grandma never set foot in school. Raised by her grandma far from her own parents, she grew up to be a successful woman. After running from a forced marriage to an old man, she married a schoolteacher and went on to become a powerful lady, versed in investment and real estate, and giving back to her community. She taught me not only the basic things a woman needs to know, but more importantly, how to stand up for my dream. She was already telling me at the age of seven how to build the habit of saving a portion of my pocket money and what type of areas were worth investing in when I grow up. She has gone to rest in peace too soon, but her teachings, principles, guidance, & advice continue to accompany me on my journey.

Being a product of many nests:

I am a product of at least seven nests. My first nest was when I stayed with my grandaunt, Soumai, when I was around the age of three.

My mother went to her house to give birth to my brother and left me there when she returned home. After one year, I moved back with my parents (my second nest). I started to live in my third nest at the age of six when I left my parents to follow Coumbo Barkey to be able to go to school. At twelve years old, I was sent to a boarding school managed by the Sisters of the Immaculate Conception, my fourth nest. Although this choice to leave was not mine and adapting to this new environment was difficult mixed with children from different horizons, different faiths, different habits and discipline, I am grateful for this journey that shaped my whole life, particularly my beliefs and openness to all faiths.

I stayed in this boarding school for four years, going out every two weeks on weekends. In the interim, my adoptive mum got married and left for China. and my grandmother moved to Bobo Dioulasso, the second biggest city in Burkina Faso. So, when I would check out of boarding school during the weekend, I would stay with my aunt and her husband, my fifth nest. When I left boarding school, I moved in with them during the school year, and on holidays, I would join my grandmother in Bobo Dioulasso. This arrangement continued for six years.

A few months after I started university, despite being in the same city, I moved out and rented a two-room bachelor flat, my sixth nest. From that day, I lived alone till I graduated as a water sciences and technologies engineer and moved in with my husband, my seventh nest. Becoming a water sciences and technologies engineer was not in my plan. I wanted to become a pilot (remember my dream of flying high in the sky), but I would have had to study abroad, which was expensive: I didn't have the means to finance that. After my graduation from high school, I got a scholarship from my government to study in the faculty of Sciences and Geology, which was not my first choice, so I tried my best to join another faculty without success. Hence, I pursued geology against my will but ended up loving the minerals, the shape of rocks, the mysteries of volcanoes and groundwater. After my bachelor's degree in geology, I got another scholarship and admission to pursue a master's degree in mineralogy at Limoges, France. I was excited and sold the little furniture I had in my flat, but because it was during the revolution era, one week before the trip, our government blocked all students from going abroad.

Despite my pain and anger, and after a well-deserved short break, I returned to my faculty to pursue a master's degree in hydrogeology.

This is how I became a water sciences and technologies engineer, and thirteen years later, returned to do a PhD in freshwater ecology. This winding study path ironically brought me closer to something I had loved for a long time, but had never envisioned working with or in, water. I went from seeing water as a ground for leisure, contemplation and comfort to understanding its system and cycles, doing my best to help countries manage and protect this precious resource. I am grateful that I ended up working in the field of water and ecosystems, which also allows me to fly in the sky, even if it is not in the pilot's seat.

Our paradigm does shape our lives and our decisions. My whole life changed because of education. I jumped from nest to nest for education. Having been left, been out on my own, and having witnessed many other people moving around, I guess I was prepared to accept that leaving is a natural process for me. Even when I started my career, I was always on the move, the one leaving, traveling a lot, and coming back to the "nest". My husband was the one staying most of the time with the children, as he was traveling less, although he, too, had a very demanding business.

In 2007, within the framework of my job, I left my home country and family for the first time to work internationally in Tunis. I was alone, and it was lonely, so much so that I refused to renew my contract after one year. I was so depressed, and I would cross out a day on my wall calendar whenever I left the office. Going home every three months didn't help. I returned home even though I didn't have a job waiting for me.

After a year, I joined the United Nations and move to Bamako, Mali to work internationally. This time, I asked my children and husband to help me decide. Since Bamako was not too far from home, I went alone again but I returned home every month, and my family visited every school holiday. The arrangement was difficult but manageable during the three years I spent in Bamako.

A dramatic change happened in 2012. I moved to Nairobi. I was happy I had the children with me this time, as the distance between Nairobi and Ouagadougou was too far to make regular trips, and they were also entering their teenage years. Further, moving to Nairobi offered an opportunity for them to master English. My husband decided to stay in Burkina Faso. In fact, writing this book opened my mind to how hard this move was on my husband, seeing his whole family leaving. I still feel guilty for having made him go through this, even though the situation was not based on selfishness, but to give our children the opportunity to see the world, embrace the English language and prepare them for a better future. So, in July 2012, the children and I moved to Nairobi: new city, new environment, new weather, new job, new colleagues, different language, different way of driving. (In Burkina Faso, we drive on the right side of the road).

One month later, my older daughter Kenny left for university in Montreal where she had been accepted. Seeing her leave was painful, and I felt emptiness, but I still had two children to care for. To go abroad was Kenny's decision and also our decision, as parents, to give her this opportunity. Indeed, from the start, we made the decision that our children would go abroad for university to give them more opportunities for success. We also let them decide what they wanted to do and where they wanted to study. Hence, Kenny, at the age of eighteen, was the first to leave the nest. Although seeing her leave was painful, based on my paradigm and my story, I put education first, so the pain did not change the decision. Montreal was not the first time my daughter traveled alone. She traveled alone or with her siblings during school holidays to visit her grandmother in France. However, Canada was far away, and she was not going for holidays but moving there. She had to face a new city, a new continent, the Canadian winter, find accommodation, deal with administration, etc., and still perform academically. We supported her financially, but she had to do everything else alone. She had to overcome a big challenge—and she did! I am so proud of her today.

We all had to adjust. For example, I had to learn how to drive on the left, and it wasn't easy. I recall one day I was with my younger daughter, and we went to visit a couple who had a baby. We parked the car in an underground garage with lots of pillars. When the time to leave came, we got into the car, and I tried to drive out. I bumped into a pillar, and my daughter got out of the car to see what happened. "Po, Po, Po . . . You're lucky Daddy isn't here to see this!"

I was intrigued and gave her a glime (a sideways glance), then got out of the car. I saw that one side was heavily damaged. "I wish your dad was here so I wouldn't have to drive, and I wouldn't have to take this car to a garage to fix it."

Indeed, having to deal alone with juggling the job, finding accommodation, a school for the children, and taking care of them was difficult, and I deeply felt the void of my husband's absence. He used to wake up earlier and prepare breakfast and snacks for the children on school days. A simple thing like changing a bulb or checking what was going on during a black-out (something that happens often in Nairobi) or starting a stubborn car in the morning, reminded me of the importance of having someone who cares nearby.

Adapting to the new environment was also difficult for my son, Keith, and my daughter, Kolene. Even though they were going to the French school, they had to learn and master English and be aware of the security issue in Nairobi. Without their father being with us in Nairobi, managing these two teenagers was challenging, but it helped all of us bond.

Keith's leaving for Kedge Business School in Bordeaux in 2015 was painful, and I was worried. Was he really ready to be on his own? Would he wake up on time for class? Would he manage to stick to the values we, as parents, gave him? But I had to let go and learn to trust in his ability to choose what was best for him. He ended up performing well and, doing several school exchanges: first in Ottawa, Canada; then in Shanghai, China; and finally in Seoul, South Korea before graduating. He went through his own journey, overcame the challenges he encountered, and we are so proud today of the young man he has grown up to be.

Kolene and I readjusted ourselves—or so I thought. After two years, we moved to a new house, unfortunately far from her school, and made new plans for both of us. I consoled myself that I still had more years with her before she left. Then she decided to leave one year early: Was she feeling lonely because her siblings left? Was she having difficulty with their departure? She was so close to her brother . . . I was not ready to let her go.

I fought, objected, and gave up when I realized this was what she wanted to do. So, I helped her find a boarding school in Hamilton, Canada. Taking her to a boarding school was more for my own peace of mind as she wanted to go to Toronto and live with her sister, but Hamilton was the compromise. I helped her settle in, then came back to Nairobi. Going around empty bedrooms in a house with no sounds, no messes, and no one to call or talk to, no one to hug, was awful. The nest was completely empty. It was then that I really felt the emptiness.

As I said, the empty nest has been harder for my husband who found himself in an empty nest all in one day, without children and a wife. Although emptying the nest was gradual for me, it hasn't been easy. To understand that the nest is empty doesn't take long: you drop your child at the airport and return home to see an empty room, —the beginning of many moments of feeling something is missing; — the chaos in the bedroom, the messy kitchen, the empty place at the dinner table, the friends visiting, the laughter.

That I had a demanding job, traveled a lot and engaged in social activities while at the same time taking care of my children, lessened the feeling of emptiness when they left. I was building my career and had many personal projects and plans for the future, so I re-focused my time on those.

What this means for you is that to acknowledge what is happening is important. Think about the situation even if it is unpleasant. Reflecting on what sustains your decision as it will help you. At one time, you left your family yourself, either to pursue a career or build a family. You have to face the facts; you cannot bury your head in the sand. In this process, you must take the time to think through what is happening. You might not be happy about the way you feel right now, but how do you make the best of this present situation? Your decision-making process can help you find a suitable coping mechanism. To acknowledge the feelings is important. Don't brush things under the rug. Think the situation through and identify exactly what you are afraid of.

The situation can be different depending on whether you are a stay-home parent or you have a full-time job. Many parents told me that focusing on their careers was the best coping mechanism that helped them navigate through the situation. Having another interest area on which to focus your time and energy will help stave off depression or that sense of loss.

The feeling of loneliness or emptiness may come quickly or at a later stage. Once the novelty of a new situation wears off is when the feelings of loneliness begin to settle in. While you are busy getting admission for your child and planning, you are in the process, on the move, and you don't really know what it'll be like once they leave the house.

In any case, what is important is to recognize the feeling, assess the situation and embrace the change. Accepting what is happening is the first step, followed by processing the mourning without getting lost in it. The more you focus on feelings of uselessness and loneliness, the more you will drown. Learn how to bounce back and swim.

The situation could provide you with more time on your hands. This could be the opportunity to explore other activities that can give you meaning and purpose.

Remembering the different roles, you had in life in addition to being a parent and clarifying the ones you would like to take on now may help you bounce back and strengthen your sense of self-worth. I learned five steps to develop a resilience pathway in one of the programs I mentioned earlier:

- Nurture yourself by prioritizing your mental and physical health.

- Look for opportunities for personal growth and self-discovery.

- Learn to accept that change is part of life: how do I handle change? Resist? Accept?

- Take decisive action rather than give in to passivity and withdrawal.

- Learn from the past, and view challenges as opportunities for growth.

INSTANT ACTION STEP

Take five minutes right now to think through the situation and assess your feelings.

How do you make the best use of this present situation?

What are the five actions you can start taking today?

SECRET #2

ADJUST AND EMBRACE YOUR MANY OTHER ROLES.

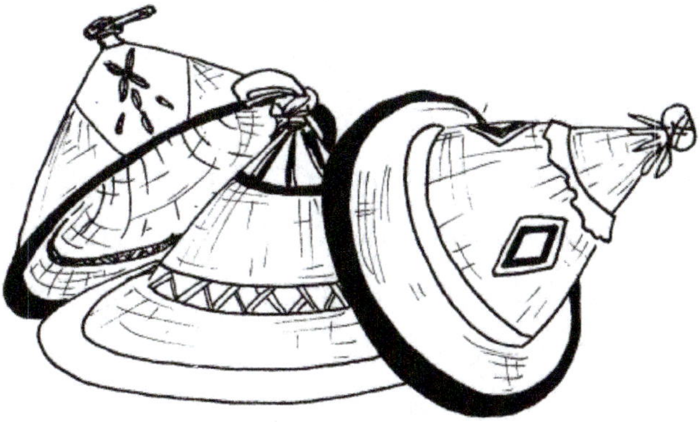

"All the world's a stage,
And all the men and women merely players;
They have their exits and their entrances,
And one man in his time plays many parts,
His acts being seven ages."
—William Shakespeare, As You Like It.

The empty nest can create an upheaval in parents' lives or, on the contrary, a more enriching, productive, and creative time by reviving the relationship with one's partner. The empty nest may renew old friendships and hobbies, thus continuing personal growth and fostering the perception of a new adventure for development rather than a loss[3].

You were once a child in a family. You left and became a partner, and then, if you so chose, a parent. Once you have children, you adjust your life to welcome them, and you reorganize your life around them. In this process, the focus can remain on your marriage or shift to your children. In any case, children will occupy an important place in your life. Thus, you feel the void when they leave, and you might see yourself at times as useless. You tend to forget that you play other roles in society, e.g., child, sister, brother, colleague, spouse, etc.

Psychologist Donald E. Super devised "The Life Career Rainbow" and explained the concept in his book, The Psychology of Careers (Harper, 1957).

---

[3]Kaur, Mandeep & Kaur Jaismeen, 2021. The reality therapy: a boon to recuperate from empty nest syndrome. International Journal of Choice Theory and Reality Therapy; Manhattan. Vol.40 Iss.2, (Spring 2021): 46-62.

He modified the concept in 1980 to address different career development paths by identifying eight roles you play throughout your life (Child, Student, Leisurite, Citizen, Worker, Parent, Spouse, and Homemaker) and five "life stages" during which you devote more or less time to each role.

These life roles come and go over the course of your life, so being aware of all of them is important for a more harmonious self. When you allocate the appropriate amount of effort and time to your different roles, you have a balanced life. Understanding the patterns of the different roles will help you prepare for life's changes. Becoming a parent, retirement, and children leaving home are tremendous life events that require role change on your part. We all play multiple roles in life. Once a role becomes less important, we have to think of its replacement amid the shifting level of importance of the other roles.

Keeping a journal throughout the different stages of your life can help you recognize when to shift and adjust. I can list many personal shifts: engineer, geologist environmentalist, yogi, coach, coachee, spouse, parent, daughter, sister, volunteer, colleague, writer, mentor, teammate, provider, etc.

While researching the subject, I found PRICE, a mnemonic life coach bloggers[4] use to group the life roles into five categories:

- *Professional*
- *Relatives (family, friends)*
- *Inner-Self (intrapersonal/knowing yourself)*
- *Citizen (community, religion, social group, etc.)*
- *Environment (your surroundings, nature, pollution, fresh air, etc.)*

We do indeed wear many hats and are called upon to change those hats depending on with whom we are engaged at the time of an encounter, meeting, or task. Each role comes with different expectations. As one or two roles consume most of our time, we may feel we are not reaching the expectations we set for the other roles, e.g., being so dedicated to our jobs that we fail as a parent, or being so consumed by work and parenthood that we disconnect from friends and extended family. To understand that our multiple roles are interconnected is crucial. Try to unify them, allowing different roles to coexist in harmony in one being. For this to happen, we need to see ourselves as one whole person and accept all our roles.

---

[4] Life Coach Bloggers : https://lifecoachbloggers.blogspot.com/2016/04/Roles-life-list- Accessed, October 10, 2022, 20:20

Often our different roles conflict. For example, I was president of the Leo club Doyen in Burkina Faso in 1994. I had my first child and had to leave her behind when she was nine months old. I traveled to Bingerville, Cote d' Ivoire to organize the Lions Cub Congress in 1995, lead our club, and deliver the speeches for our club. Those ten days seemed like an eternity because I was away from my baby who was still breastfeeding. To leave my daughter behind to go to the congress was difficult, but for me to honor my duty as president of my club was important, although I did so at the expense of my role as a mother. Unfortunately, this scenario is not unusual for women. Once you know what your different roles in everyday life are, you will be able to understand your needs and the needs demanded by society.

The empty nest phase is a period that promotes freedom and improved relationships, and can facilitate and promote a more mature, more emotionally meaningful and a deeper relationship for oneself and one's marital relationship[5]. Hence, this period could be an opportunity to reconnect with your spouse, improve your relationship and, at the same time, embrace the different other roles you have in society.

---

[5]Kumar P. Saleel, 2015, "Psychological Well Being and Marital Adjustment: A Study on Elderly Couples in Post Parental Stage of Life." Indian Journal of Gerontology 2015, Vol. 29, No. 1, pp. 77–90. School of Social Work, Marian College Kuttikkanam, Peermade, Kerala, India – 685 531

Nowadays, couples live apart in separate cities, countries, and even continents. Those in this situation, like me, are called "geographical singles".
However, for a couple living together, the empty nest provides time for new romance with each other. Remember before the children were born. Take time to rediscover each other, particularly, if you have centered your life around your children and neglected your marriage and romance. Even if you managed to keep a marriage-centered family, taking time to rediscover each other, invent new activities, and discover new horizons is still of vital importance. Now that the nest is empty, you need to relearn to live as just the two of you.

Other roles you play in society are also important. With the children around and your time scattered, you may not have spent enough time with siblings, friends, and colleagues who are friends outside the office. Time spent impacts the relationship you have with others. Relationships need to be built and maintained, which takes time and dedication. To cultivate satisfying relationship with others requires three vital abilities:

- *Know yourself.*
- *Be aware of others' personalities and behavior.*
- *Know different ways to manage and deal with others.*

The first ability is called intrapersonal intelligence; the latter two are called interpersonal intelligence. Both include effective verbal and non-verbal communication skills.

Develop both your intrapersonal and interpersonal intelligence to be aware of your own roles so you can either make a change, manage your roles, or decide to cherish the various roles in your life.

I had to rebuild and nurture my network. I found myself with a timetable of calls to make, friends to visit, and birthday parties and community gatherings to attend. I researched the contacts of old schoolmates and created a WhatsApp group comprised of women with whom I attended boarding school at College Notre Dame de Kologh-Naba.

I also created another WhatsApp group comprised of the twelve classmates with whom I went through university. Because we were twelve, like the European Economic Community (CEE in French) at the time, we called ourselves the CEE, and decided to keep that name for our WhatsApp group chat. Reconnecting was rewarding and brought us together to chat, laugh, and be there to support each other, to celebrate, and to pay visits to old professors. Reconnecting provides a sense of belonging and is a wonderful uplifting therapy.

I decided to reconnect with my old friends and actively rebuilt my network. It is true that friendship and networks are like flowers: they need to be planted, watered, and nurtured, or they wilt and die. I had more time to stay or meet after work and to do things before going home, e.g., going to the gym or meeting with club members.

I also became more connected with cousins, siblings, and extended family via the Internet and phone when abroad, and by spending time together when visiting my home country. To feel better, I began reading more books like I did as a child. Eventually I joined an online book club where we would decide on the books to read and meet to review chapter by chapter and share the lessons we picked up from each book.

People used to come to me for advice and counseling. Using my experience and what I learned from books and personal development courses, I mentored and coached young professionals, friends, and family members on their careers, relationships, and lives. I loved mentoring and coaching from a young age, and I increasingly appreciate the activity now that I am alone. Sometimes I get questions that inspire me to reflect and require me to research. I feel a sense of accomplishment when I help others and watch them succeed.

The way you are impacted will depend on the way you are living and acting in these different roles.
If you are a stay-at-home parent devoting all your time to managing the family—to making sure that everyone is safe and well cared for—you will feel the empty nest more. However, if you are performing your role as a parent in addition to your full-time job/an outside activity, you will likely tend to shift your focus to the job to fill the void.

Several parents I have talked with said they became more involved in church, associations, or philanthropic activities that kept them active and gave them a sense of belonging and recognition. Many possibilities exist for you to help and support others once you lift your eyes from your own bubble and look around. Further, the act of volunteering your time, money, or energy to help others not only makes the world a better place, but boosts your happiness, health, and sense of well-being.

It is up to you to decide and choose where and how you want to invest your time and energy to make you feel better. Once you decide, everything is possible. You can revive old relationships or build and nurture new ones.

You can join philanthropic services clubs, get more involved in religious groups, or simply contribute to improving the area in which you live.
Nowadays technology makes it easy to reconnect. Imagine how we would have coped during Covid without the incredible technological developments—with no mobile phones, no Internet, and only faxes and letters. Today, even at an altitude of 30,000 miles, we can stay connected. Thus, adjust and embrace the many roles we are so blessed to have.

INSTANT ACTION STEP

Take five minutes right now to list the different roles you play in your life.

How are you filling them?

Do you spend equal time in each? Quality time?

What are two actions you can start doing today to adjust your life and embrace the other roles you have?

SECRET #3

TAKE TIME FOR FITNESS AND WELL-BEING.

"It is health that is real wealth and not pieces of gold and silver."
_Mahatma Gandhi

Sport was never my thing! In high school, I excelled in all disciplines except sports—the only subject where I was sure to fail the class. I was flexible, but I was not good at running, climbing, jumping or any other physical activities.

My asthma would act up, so I could not sleep at night because of difficulty breathing. Nevertheless, the nuns insisted I participate, making my classmates happy at the opportunity to beat me in a subject.

It was only when I went to high school at College de La Salle that the Brothers of the Christian Schools' understood my asthma and recommended I swim when others were doing different sports. I fell in love with swimming; the sport was a turning point for me that I still enjoy. In university, I spent Sundays at the swimming pool. Apart from dancing and swimming, which were dear hobbies, I dropped all sports from my life as soon as I could make that decision for myself.

Life went on, and I continued to enjoy dancing and swimming alone or at the sports center with friends. I always kept active, even during pregnancy and despite having a full-time job. However, when I accepted a job at the African Development Bank and moved to Tunis, I stopped dancing and swimming. The job was too demanding, and I was lonely. I experienced for the first time what it meant to live without my husband and children. I stayed a year, but it was difficult. I missed my family so much that I felt depressed and had to cut my contract short. At that time, I was diagnosed with a cholesterol issue.

The recommendation was to do sports or take pills: I chose sports over pills and started walking a minimum of thirty minutes a day. Sports gradually became part of my routine— first walking, then I joined a gym club and became a regular. This regimen continued and helped me cope when I went to work for the United Nations in Bamako, Mali as within walking distance from my house, I quickly found a sports club that I frequented daily.

The UN complex in Nairobi offered a perfect setting to embrace physical activities. However, when I first moved there, I was busy settling into this new environment with my children, so, once again, I stopped exercising. A routine checkup revealed that my bad cholesterol was kicking in again, and pills were prescribed. I took them for one week before deciding to drop them and return to sports. I went to the UN recreation center, a sports and leisure facility, and was astounded at all they offered—near the office. I enrolled and started walking, swimming, and dancing (my first love), and later embraced yoga and Pilates.

Adding these new activities to my already full schedule (job, parenting) was challenging. I was busy with all these physical activities and traveling, too. When my children were home, I chose an activity schedule that corresponded with their schedule and the time we needed to be home together. Once they left, this criterion became irrelevant since, except for our beloved dog Chamallow, I had no one waiting for me, so time was no longer a constraint.

I intensified my practice from two to three times a week to a daily routine and added new disciplines such as Pilates and African dance.
The exercise relieved office stress kept the cholesterol under control, and exhausted me enough to make me crave my bed when I returned to the empty house in the evening. (I would leave the house early in the morning and return in time to have dinner and go to bed.) Sport became not only a habit but an escape. At first, I did not realize I immersed myself in sports, keeping myself busy seven days a week, as a coping mechanism for my loneliness.

In 2020, when the world pandemic Covid-19 started spreading and the world went into a global quarantine, we had to work from home. The closing of the recreation center was dramatic. I don't know how I would have survived if my young sister, Sadjo, had not arrived in Nairobi three days before the lockdown. With virtual meetings the norm, having someone to talk to in person was a relief. With the recreation center closed, we went for long walks in the countryside since I was fortunate to live on the border of the city, in Redhill, amongst tea plantations and small streams. Nairobi is beautiful.

What does this recounting mean for you?

You can never be too late to embrace physical activity. You don't need to engage in Olympic speed training or have been a good athlete. All you need is the resolve to start, continue, and resume whenever you find yourself off track. Exercise changes not only your body but also your mind, attitude, and mood.

If you were already doing physical activities before the children left the nest, now that they are gone, you have more time to continue prior programs and enroll in an exciting new discipline. If you were not physically active when the children were home, start with baby steps, e.g., walking thirty minutes each day. If you love swimming as I do, include this disciple in your routine wherever possible. Make yoga your companion. Learn African or Latin dances. There is so much to discover and enjoy!

Doing all these activities was easy when I lived in Nairobi, as I had access to all of them at the recreation center next to my office. When I moved to Bonn, I realized how difficult it could be to find one place with all the facilities. I understand now that a huge part of why people are not physically active is the lack of access to fitness facilities. The good news is that yoga, dance classes, and workouts are available on YouTube. If you don't have nearby access to a swimming pool, be advised that you will need discipline and willpower to continue swimming, first by finding a pool and paying the cost. I finally found one, not far from my house, but I struggle to get back to my weekly swimming exercises.

A healthy diet is important on this journey. As the saying goes, to be fit, one needs to fix the food first. Two things happen when you find yourself alone: either you improve your diet, or you slip into junk food. The latter is the easiest route and one to which you must pay attention. You might be cooking to please your children, to prepare their preferred meals to see the smiles on their faces when they come back from school and discover what Mummy or Daddy has made for them. If so, to cook when they leave might be difficult. I am talking about parents who cook for themselves.

If you have house help, which is common in Africa (but a luxury in Europe), you can still tell the person what to cook. When you are alone, dragging yourself to the kitchen might be difficult. Why bother? It's just you. At that moment, you need to observe what is happening, accept the situation, and refocus. If you are already following a diet and watching what you are eating (due to health reasons or because you want to keep fit), deciding what to cook is easier because you don't have to juggle among many food preferences.

Although following a healthy diet may be difficult, the benefits outweigh the challenges. A healthy diet has a positive effect on both your physical and mental health. Eating well helps with sleeping patterns and energy levels, and reduces the risk of pathologies such as heart disease and diabetes. Healthy eating helps you feel and look good. My coach always tells me, "Your body is a result of what you eat." I used to interpret that as if I eat healthily, I will look healthy. If I eat junk food, my body will reflect it. I now realize this interpretation is not true for everybody; some thin, healthy looking people have diseases, and some obese people have no disease at all. Indeed, your health, not what you see in the mirror, should be your priority when you think about what you put on your plate.

This attitude is so true of your mindset and of your life as well. Your life is a result of what you feed your Mind, Body, and Soul. Your thoughts, words, self-care, and self-talk become your reality.

Feed yourself positive thoughts, beliefs, love, faith, and happiness, and you will experience these things. Feed yourself negative thoughts, self-doubt, hate, fear, and other drama, and you will experience these things. I am not saying to shift from negative thoughts to positive ones is easy, but shifting is a muscle that can be built. Self-development books, meditation and practices teach many techniques that help us think positively.

Human minds are in constant turmoil with approximately 80,000 thoughts per day, which make our minds difficult to control. For this reason, the Japanese healing practice Reiki teaches us to learn to let go instead of trying to control. Negative thinking tends to exaggerate everything, especially bad events. Since you cannot use a switch to stop your thoughts, you need to learn tips to help you become more positive gradually. This change cannot happen suddenly but requires being aware and conscious of your thoughts. Techniques such as breathing and relaxation help shift our way of thinking so that our positive thoughts outweigh the negative. I find listening to music, morning affirmations, and evening reflections on the "little joys" I experienced during the day to be helpful in shifting my thoughts toward positivity. First, acknowledge the negative thoughts by accepting you have them, and then decide what to do with them.

Rehashing dark ideas can be exhausting, so write down these thoughts before objectively examining them and listing the different scenarios from worst to the best. This format will help you realize what is more likely to happen. Step-by-step, when you find yourself dwelling on negative thoughts, mentally acknowledge, pause, and rephrase your thoughts. Gradually you will embrace the habit of seeing setbacks as temporary and specific rather than as permanent and pervasive, and you will stop over-generalizing the negative. Imagination is a wonderful tool if used constructively but not if used to scare yourself. To stop negative thinking takes time and requires continuous effort.

I encourage you to dream bigger, believe in yourself and enjoy your journey to greatness. Know that in this journey to greatness, being physically fit and mentally sound are your winning chess pawns.

INSTANT ACTION STEP

Take five minutes to reflect on fitness and well-being.

What do these mean for you?

Do you consider yourself fit and comfortable, healthy, and happy?

Or do you need to do something about you physical and mental state?

What is one action you can start doing from today?

SECRET #4

RE-DISCOVER YOUR PASSION AND FIND YOUR LIFE'S PURPOSE.

"'Every human being has a gift of genius and a personal calling encoded in them from birth. It is up to you to discover it, to develop it, to own it, and to share this gift with the world. This is your life's purpose."
_Oprah Winfrey

Human beings want to find their purpose in life to feel fulfilled. Sometimes we confuse our purpose with our achievements, like being tennis world champion, getting married, having children, or having a successful career.

These achievements often do not bring the fulfillment that comes with finding your personal sense of purpose.
A life's purpose goes beyond these preconceived ideas. A personal sense of purpose is your compass that guides you and keeps you moving no matter the obstacles or setbacks you face. This is also why finding your purpose is essential for living a happy, healthy life. Purpose is your why; it's what keeps you awake at night and even makes you cry. Finding the answer to this question can unlock greater satisfaction and success in all areas of your life.

We all have a set of talents and interests that light us up and make us jump out of bed every morning. Although some get out of bed due to responsibility and may argue they don't have talent or interests, I am yet to be convinced there isn't something in this life that they prefer above all. For parents who may have spent years waking up at odd hours because of parental responsibilities—burying their passion to focus on the responsibility—sometimes just trying to survive, is easy. Still, it does not mean they haven't any talents or interests.

Your passion and interests are a good indicator of where your life-purpose lies. Often what you are passionate about, what brings you joy, is what you can contribute to the world. Both are interconnected. Using your gifts to serve others can help you find your true purpose. Thus, you craft your sense of purpose from your passion as well as from practical considerations based on what the world needs. While passion is about you and what you love doing, purpose is about how to serve others. In other words, passion reflects you, while purpose is directed at serving others' interests. Aligning passion and purpose can seem daunting, but getting to know yourself is the starting point.

The route to self-discovery can be a long roller-coaster ride, but it is a journey worth taking. As far as I can remember, I have always tried to improve in all aspects of my life. I was born in a small village. My parents lost their first child, a girl, and then the second, a boy. As a result, they had me undergo different rituals and beliefs to keep me alive by keeping the "bad spirit" away. Many of the rituals changed for their subsequent children. For example, they didn't shave my head according to our custom for newborns until I started walking, nor did they follow the custom for my siblings. Part of these rituals included piercing my brothers' ears and having them wear a cauri shell on one ear, which is not usual.

Despite being born into a Muslim family, I attended Catholic schools, which then and now have the best reputation. This experience gave me an open mind about religions. I would add that this situation is not uncommon in Burkina Faso, which does not focus on religious disparities. Ironically, as a little Muslim girl, I knew the Bible better than the Holy Qur'an but that didn't stop me from remaining a practicing Muslim. In my quest to become a better version of myself in all aspects of my life, I was curious and eager to understand different religions and faiths (Christianity, Hinduism, Buddhism, Judaism . . .)

I left my parents at a very early age to go to school. When I learned to read, reading became a passion. I had few friends at school; books were my friends. I read all the children's categories. In high school, I read romance books, but then shifted to all kinds of books and dove into personal development books.

A book helps readers see the world, live many vicarious experiences, discover possibilities, & shape thinking.

As a hungry learner, reading has always helped me fill these needs. That I always wanted to become a better version of myself drove me to be the best student in my class and to work to improve my attitude by fixing myself. I enrolled in online courses aimed at learning new languages, training in leadership & management, diving into spirituality.... while mentoring others who asked for my advice and guidance.

I am inclined to all aspects of personal development. These two words can be overwhelming & sometimes confusing as they can become a tote, carrying all aspects of our life: mental, social, spiritual, emotional, and physical. Personal development is a lifelong process that serves as a way for us to assess our skills, consider our aims in life, and set goals in order to realize our potential. My journey has been long and is ongoing. From a relatively young age, I was inclined to spirituality and personal growth.

For example, my first investment when I received my university scholarship was buying books on hypnosis and telepathy. Personal development entails a long process of starting, stopping, and resuming—but never giving up.

The well-known mystic Yogi, Sadhguru, defines spirituality as a quest, a longing to know, an intense expression in the form of seeking. Spirituality is not a religion. Being spiritual means, you are in touch with your own deep self.

When writing this book, I reached out and interviewed my former boss at the United Nations Environment Programmed (UNEP), Vincent Sweeney, a wonderful human being. I was stunned by what he said:

"I wonder how people can live without that part of their life—I mean, spirituality not being a part of their life. It would be so empty without having someone to turn to . . . We think it's hard to believe in a Higher Being, but I would find it hard to not, to be honest, at this stage of my life. When you're younger, you feel more in control of everything around you, that everything is in your hands, the world is your playground, and you can determine what will happen. As you get older, you become much humbler, surprisingly, and realize that things are not in your hands. What we thought we had control of, we may realize we have no control of, and we have to submit."

Indeed, having something or someone to turn to in moments of pain but also in moments of joy is important. For me, religion and spirituality constitute the base that helps me bounce and carry on.

Myriads of diverse religions & spiritual beliefs abound alive & vibrant around the world. They provide a sense of peace, purpose, and forgiveness that helps their followers better handle stress and illness.

Many scientific researchers have found that spirituality plays an essential role in mental well-being and has a powerful positive effect on happiness, health, relationships[6] and physical health[7]. Hence, when faced with challenges or setbacks, spiritual people tend to cope more effectively with stress. The World Health Organization (WHO) defines mental health as "a state of wellbeing in which the individual realizes his or her abilities, can cope with the normal stresses of life, work productively and fruitfully, and is able to make a contribution to his or her community.

---

[6]Verghese A. Spirituality and mental health. Indian J Psychiatry. 2008 Oct;50(4):233-7. doi: 10.4103/0019-5545.44742. PMID: 19823605; PMCID: PMC2755140.

Paloutzian, R., and Park, C. L. (2013). Handbook of psychology of religion and spirituality. New York: Guilford Press.

Pargament, K. I., Wong, S., and Exline, J. J. (2016). "Wholeness and holiness: the spiritual dimension of eudaimonics" in Handbook of eudaimonic well-being. ed. J. Vittersø (New York: Springer Press), 379–394.; Kenneth I, Serena Wong, Julie J. Exline-2022; The Holiness of Wholeness: Religious Contributions to Human Flourishing ; 2022; Pages432–C32.P92. https://doi.org/10.1093/oxfordhb/9780190064570.013.31

[7]Koenig, H., King, D., and Carson, V. B. (2012). Handbook of Religion and Health. New York, NY: Oxford University Press.

Practices such as prayer and meditation are the common denominator of many religions and the foundation of spirituality. I made these practices my companions, and they continue to help me in my life journey.

Would my quest for self-improvement explain why I plunged into spirituality? A few years into yoga, I started meditation and focused more on personal development and practicing what I was reading. When the children left and I found myself alone, I intensified my practices. I reached a point where meditation became part of my daily routine, and I enrolled in an online course to improve my practices and eventually teach them one day. The road ahead is still long, but I am loving the journey.

My husband is neither a spiritual nor a religious person. However, he can lose himself in gardening. He wakes up early in the morning to water his flowers, feed the birds, and watch the sunrise while listening to the news. Because of his passion for flowers and plants, our home is a mini botanical garden. He will always look for the flowers/plants he does not have. When he would visit us in Nairobi, he would search for flowers native to Kenya that cannot be found in Burkina and find out how to acquire them. He also shares and advises others about their garden.

What does this mean for you? You can seek other aspects of your life that may bring you meaning and peace. Dedicating time to exploring and reigniting your passions is important, as your passions have the power to uplift and inspire you. For some, that passion could be gardening or cooking, while for others, it could be hiking or learning to speak a new language. I love reading, which led me to deepen my spiritual life.

Once you discover your inner calling, the possibilities for fulfillment are endless. You can enroll in online courses or get a coach to help you. I have a friend who, at the age of sixty-five, learned to teach downhill skiing to young children and became certified. Most parents I talked with during the process of writing this book have been practicing their religion or spiritual life more since their children left. You can also take time to travel to new places and discover the world. There is no good or bad answer. What is important for a fulfilled life is to spend time in self-reflection, find your life purpose, and fully embrace your passions. Setting a routine for self-care is also important in one's life. Self-care includes five dimensions, all equally important. Only you can find the right balance that provides you with a blissful life.

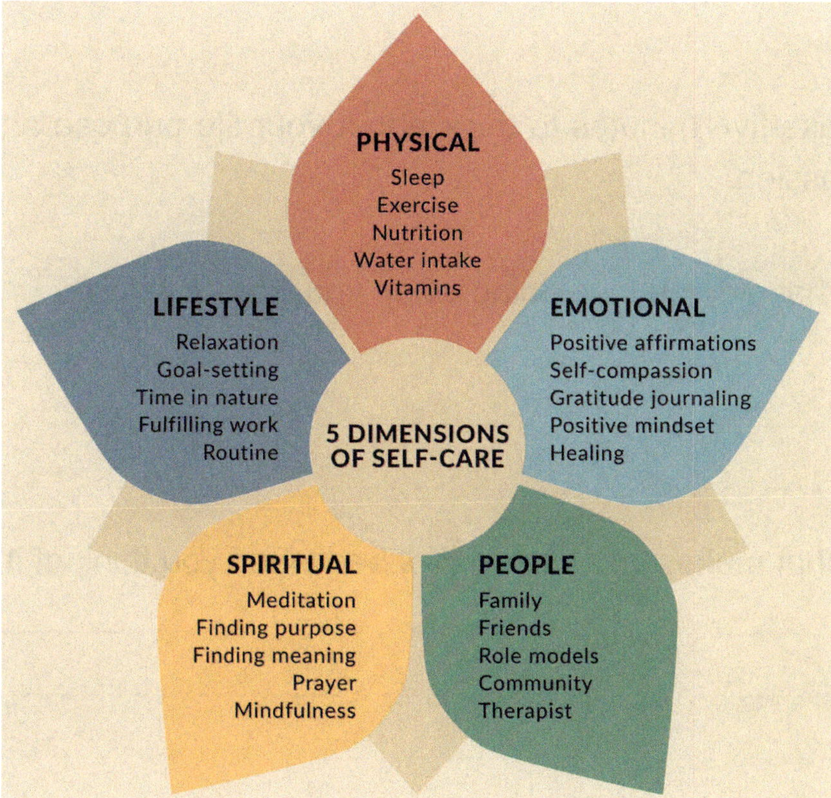

Courtesy of Agnes Cserhati, leadership development coach and trainer

INSTANT ACTION STEP

Take five minutes to think about your life purpose and passion.

What did you love doing when you were a child?

What makes you jump out of bed when you think of it?

What is that thing you can do starting today that can make you happy and fulfilled?

SECRET #5

SOCIALIZE, REVIVE, AND BUILD YOUR NETWORK.

"Treasure your relationships, not your possessions."
_Anthony J. D'Angelo

Like every human being, I went through cycles: I started as outgoing and open, and I love dancing. I recall one day when I was a preschooler, we received a griot in our village house, & I spent the whole night dancing. Each family has its griot, an important storyteller who knows, keeps, and passes on oral tradition and family lineage.

A griot is usually a praise singer, and when he praises your lineage, you are expected to reward him. The griot profession is hereditary and has long been a part of West African cultures.
The griot’s role has traditionally been to preserve people's genealogies, historical narratives, and oral traditions. Each time a family receives a griot is an opportunity for almost three nights of cultural events during which people gather to listen to him and dance. Being a cute young party animal, I could always be found among the dancers who would spend the whole night dancing.

Growing up, I became shy and was always looking for a quiet place to lose myself in books. At boarding school, we had cultural nights during which students would present dance performances. As I loved music and dance, I enjoyed rehearsing with my friends but was too shy to perform onstage in front of the public. After boarding school, I listened to music and danced every day in my room, but I was still shy.

The boarding school, with its outdoor activities and associated clubs such as the World Association of Girl Guides and Girl Scouts helped me to open up and overcome my shyness. These groups gave me an opportunity to meet peers, learn to help those in need in society, and develop leadership, organizational and social skills. In pursuing the same objective, I later joined the Leo club, a service club and the younger version of the Lions Club International. The Leo club is a global family of young people where I volunteered my time and money to improve the lives of others. Joining the Leo club was beneficial in helping me grow as an individual and as a leader. I immersed myself in helping organize galas, fundraisers, and donations to raise funds for orphanages, widow associations, hospitals, and the most vulnerable in our society. These activities are the heart and soul of club life for every Lions Club worldwide. Lions and Leos are ordinary people from all walks of life who give their time freely to serve their community and beyond through support and aid.

Before leaving when I reached thirty years old, I served in different positions in my Leo club: secretary, liaison officer with the Lions Club, vice-president, president and past president.

These different roles allowed me to develop my abilities as an organizer, time manager, and peer motivator, effectively building my leadership skills. Being part of the Leo organization was fulfilling and uplifting; I was with like-minded people, supporting those in need through humanitarian services and grants that impact lives globally, & encouraging peace and international understanding. We also had lots of fun traveling together.

The Leo club has left an imprint on my life.
The passion to serve others burns within me. Hence, I continue to engage in different associations and clubs, to volunteer my time, and to involve myself in education to help my community by supporting girls and boys in going to school and in efforts to build schools. As I was busy establishing my career and family so my time was limited, I did not join the Lions Club until 2020 after my children left.

Volunteering was part of my life starting in my school years. I have continued volunteering in my social and professional life. The American Heritage Dictionary of the English Language (4th edition) defines voluntarism as “the use of, or reliance on, voluntary action to maintain an institution, carry out a policy or achieve an end.” In this context, the word voluntary action means action based on free will, which in turn means action performed free from certain constraints and with no expectation of payment. Thus, volunteerism is the principle of donating time and energy to benefit other people in the community as a social responsibility rather than for any financial reward.

Volunteering is generally considered an altruistic activity intended to promote self-esteem and improve quality of life. In return, this activity can produce a feeling of self-worth and respect. No financial gain is involved. Volunteering is also renowned for skill development, socialization, and fun.

Ultimately, who benefits from volunteerism? With busy lives, finding time to volunteer can be hard. However, the benefits are enormous to an individual, to his or her family, and to the community. Volunteerism can help an individual find friends, reach out to the community, learn new skills, and even advance one's career. Volunteering helps protect mental health by building self-esteem and even physical health as the activities keep people moving. Despite what people often perceive, volunteering benefits the individual more than the cause to which the person is contributing. While volunteering is not remunerated, I often heard: Volunteers are not paid—not because they are worthless, but because they are priceless. I can attest that volunteering is a great way to socialize and build a solid, like-minded network.

Throughout this journey, I built a solid network that I revived not only for fun but also to contribute to society by doing meaningful things together. When the children left, I fully re-engaged in social life, which was significant in helping me cope with the empty nest experience.

As you reflect on your life experiences,
you may realize that you have built a vast network of colleagues, acquaintances, and friends over the years, some of whom you have known since kindergarten. At each stage of your life, you have had the opportunity to meet and connect with new people, adding to the richness & diversity of your personal and professional relationships. You have forgotten the existence of some, maintained sporadic contact with others, and a number have become friends or close friends. Mapping this network and reconnecting with like-minded people is worthwhile. You might have thought about reconnecting but never had time to reach out. Now that the children are gone, you have more time to reconnect with schoolmates and attend family's, friends', and colleagues' functions without time constraints.

You can revive or start building your network by meeting new people & building relationships. Meeting new people can be difficult compared with when you were younger since putting your trust in someone new and investing fully in them as a friend can be challenging. As you age, you will get a better sense of who you are and who you want to surround you. You will also notice your circle of friends shrinks. You will value the quality of friendship over the quantity of friends. As Oprah Winfrey said:

Surround yourself with only people who are going to lift you higher. If you are surrounded by negativity, look for a better environment.

Given the importance of friendship and social life for our emotional and physical health, investing in building the social support system we truly need is worthwhile. Nowadays, technology, particularly the Internet, has become a powerful tool enabling people of all ages to connect, from reuniting with family to catching up with old friends or making new friends. If gym or books are not your interests, look for—or start—a movie, photography, or cooking club. One way to meet people is by joining these clubs or, as I mentioned, by volunteering with a local nonprofit group or finding a church or other spiritual community.
Building a social support system eventually becomes an intentional action in which you need to invest energy and time to nurture the relationships you have. Different types of support systems for which we might need support are emotional (expression of empathy and feelings), self-esteem (confidence in one's personal worth), informational (advice and information), and instrumental (tangible aid & service) [8].

---

[8] https://www.med.upenn.edu/hbhe4/part3-ch9-key-constructs-social-support.shtml- Health behavior and health education, Theory, research and practice. Consulted 18/05/2023 at 10:36pm.

We need to identify the primary area in our life that needs strengthening as well as areas in which we can support others. The area could be one or all of them; decide which area/areas you need to strengthen. Once you have decided, use a common hobby to connect with others for mutual support. Indeed, for each hobby you enjoy, you can find others who enjoy it, too.

A shared hobby makes for a natural starting point for friendships and good relationships that are a crucial basis for a social support system. You may discover that some people seem naturally skilled in building relationships. Regardless, relationship building is a skill that can be learned. Being a good listener has been found to be an essential quality in building good relationships. People appreciate a good listener, and that strengthens the meaning of a relationship.

Tips on how to be a good LISTENER for a long-lasting relationship:

LISTEN without interrupting—
—even when you know more than the person talking to you!

LISTEN to understand.

Good listening is hearing what people actually think, mean, or feel, not what you imagine they should think, mean, or feel. Instead of guessing, politely ask:

Do I understand you correctly? Do you mean…? Are you feeling…?

Don't assume ; verify.

Avoid rushing to conclusions.

Listen without judging. If what they say does not add up, keep LISTENING.

When you hear more, what they are saying may make sense.

Refrain from putting others on the defensive.

Listen without correcting, countering, or devaluing. Otherwise, you will damage open communication.

Accept others' perceptions and feelings as the valid expressions of a valued person.

Validate the speaker by showing genuine interest. Ask probing questions. Ask the person to help you understand. "Given what you have told me, I can see why you feel that way." Empathy will increase their willingness to consider your views and accept your solutions.

Being a good listener requires a certain discipline. The hardest part about being disciplined is not the actions but making up your mind that your long-term desires are more important than your temporary cravings. However, once you learn to take control of your mind, you can literally control anything.

Be careful. You can deflate or hurt someone with what you say. Some people you meet each day need an emotional lift, so encourage them. Don't be the kind of person who pounces on a weakness in someone. Build people up and you will build yourself up. Indeed, we handle our relationship problems in one of three ways: flee, fight, or forgive. Some choose to flee. They leave the relationship and start again elsewhere—and are surprised when the condition resurfaces in the next relationship. Others fight.
Their relationships become combat zones. Stress becomes a way of life. If you want a long-lasting relationship, forgiveness should be your approach.

INSTANT ACTION STEP

Take five minutes right now to list your friends and associations or clubs with which you are OR you're familiar.

Do you feel reconnecting with/reaching out to them is worthwhile?

Or is building new relationships worthwhile?

How do you make the best use of this present situation?

What are the five actions you can do starting today?

SECRET #6

DEDICATE TIME FOR STRESS-FREE TRAVEL.

"The world is a book, and those who do not travel read only one page."
_St. Augustine of Hippo

I love flying above the clouds. The experience of being above the clouds shows me the wonders of nature.

Traveling adds new perspectives and dimensions to our lives and is beneficial to our health in that it reduces everyday stress by breaking our daily routine. When we travel, we immerse ourselves in new surroundings and experiences that can be good for our health. Travel exposes us to new ideas and ways of life that are different from what we knew growing up. While traveling has many benefits, it is often expensive and challenging to organize for the whole family. Therefore, one advantage of an empty nest is the return of easier travel. Indeed, reasons exist to believe that becoming an empty nester could provide extra time to travel as well as offer a potential increase of your travel budget due to a reduced family[9].

Traveling is one of my passions. I love discovering new countries, new cities, news seas and oceans—all the better if I can swim in those waters or at least put my feet in. I am a globe trotter. I fully embrace my nomadic Fulani—or Peulh—heritage.

The Fulani people, also known as Fulbe, are the largest nomadic ethnic group found in more than twenty nations in a wide swath of Africa, from Mauritania and Senegal to Ethiopia and Sudan. The Fulani traditionally gather around the pulaaku (Fulani way of being), a code of conduct and ethics based on restraint, endurance, wisdom, and bravery, which every Fulani has to respect.

---

[9]Piper, Alan T. (2021) : An economic analysis of the empty nest syndrome: What the leaving child does matters. SOEP papers on Multidisciplinary Panel Data Research, No. 1119, Deutsches Institut für Wirtschaftsforschung (DIW), Berlin

Fulani people are proud of their cultural heritage and would die for their dignity to avoid shame. They are known for their nomadic lifestyle as they travel in search of pasture and water to feed their cattle. Today, many have become settled or semi- nomadic.

When I was a child, I returned to my village during school holidays and would travel with my parents from one camp to another, following our cattle. The day after school closed in July, my cousin and I were sent to the village, sometimes for several months, and would return just a week before school resumed. Village life was not easy as there was no electricity, no running water and no cooking gas. During our stay in the village, we would walk long distances to fetch water or go to the bush to collect firewood. Pounding the millet and living without electricity were difficult. The only food was milk and fufu (cooked millet dipped in baobab leaves sauce). Despite the challenging conditions, we were happy and learned so much, from building the nomad huts and weaving the stem mat and decorative objects in straw and raffia, to milking the cow and cooking traditional dishes. Getting to the village on the unpaved road was arduous.
July & August are the rainy months in Burkina Faso, and often, the vehicle would get stuck. For a distance less than fifty kilometers, we could spend the whole

day traveling. One day, we had to sleep under a tree while waiting for the vehicle to be repaired. After the village, I sometimes would travel by train to Bobo Dioulasso, the second largest city in Burkina Faso, where my grandmother lived.
Despite these challenges, I enjoyed moving around to see my relatives and family during the holidays.

The first time I flew in a plane was to discover Paris when I was fifteen. I was amazed flying high above the clouds, fulfilling my childhood dream. The experience opened my mind to all that is out there, waiting to be discovered.

As a teen, I worked summer jobs, saved my allowance, and combined those two streams of income to travel. My savings allowed me to visit all the countries neighboring Burkina Faso. Being a member of the Leo club offered another opportunity to travel. Indeed, traveling brought me friends and families with whom I remain close to today.

I was later blessed with a job that involved traveling. Traveling for work taught me that you can travel without getting time to see your destination city; often, you only see the road from the airport to the hotel and workshop venue before heading back to the airport! Fortunately, not all my missions were like this, so I have seen the world. My children count the countries and continents I visit, and, as of today, that count is close to 100.

I visually keep track of the places I have been on the scratch able world map my children gave me for Christmas.

To date, I work hard, dedicate time to traveling and visiting places I love including as many wellness centers as possible. It's a never-ending cycle, and I love it. I prefer traveling with my family, but most often, I am alone. I have learned to just enjoy myself, make my plans, and see the world.

I used to be always on the move, which was easier when I was single. Travel became complicated when I had children. I continued to travel but never with total peace of mind, as I was worried about how the children were doing, particularly when they were young. I spent lots of money on phone calls from hotels—no mobile phones, WhatsApp, or Skype back then. I helped them do homework via phone calls. For me, a phone was the criterion to choose a hotel, in addition to a swimming pool.

Skype and later WhatsApp made my life easy and kept me connected with my family whenever I traveled. Although the children were with their dad, and nannies and cooks helped with the household, I still had to plan for their comings and goings and buy everything needed to make sure they had enough food, etc., for while I was away.
This became increasingly stressful when I was alone with my children in Nairobi, a country where security can be an issue. I had to rely on house help to sleep over and care for them, and on a driver to pick them up for school. I put my trust in God that all would be fine.

When the children left, I rediscovered stress-free travel. I joined a travel club and enjoyed the company of like-minded travelers. To have curated, arranged travels with no hassles was such fun. For example, when I celebrated my birthday in Pretoria, South Africa, I spent the morning in a hot air balloon, and, in the afternoon, I visited the Cullinan, an underground diamond mine. When I was in Nairobi, I went to the coast monthly and enjoyed the beach.

What does this mean for you? Now that you have time and no one to take care of, you can begin to discover the world, alone or with your partner. Travel is surely the best way to reconnect, to rekindle your romance while enjoying the wonders the world has to offer. Often, traveling is mistakenly associated with a huge cost, but travel does not need to be expensive. Start discovering places in your own country and then neighboring countries before wandering far and wide. To not notice or take time to visit things that are near us is common. However, when we receive visitors and take them to see where we live, we appreciate those places. I was happily surprised to see that local tourism is well-developed in Kenya. Wherever I went, I always found nationals taking time to go on safari and enjoy their beautiful country.

Since the earliest times, humans have traveled to see what surrounds them, and in so doing discovered and mapped the world. From the explorers—aiming to conquer to expand their countries and find new trade routes and new merchandise—to simple tourists, travel has been endemic to human development. I was in the seventh grade at secondary school the first time I heard about Ibn Battuta, and I never forgot him. This greatest traveler of the Middle Age voyaged from the Middle East to Africa to Europe to Asia, a long journey of almost thirty years that covered a distance of 120,000 kilometers. After his return to Morocco, he wrote and in 1355 published one of the world's most famous travel logs. In The Rihlah, he describes the fascinating people, cultures, & places he encountered.

One quote attributed to him summarizes his feelings and the benefits of his amazing journey: “Traveling—it leaves you speechless, then turns you into a storyteller.” of Ibn Battutah

Travel helps you break your daily routine and immerses you in new surroundings and experiences leading to new growth and wisdom. Now that you have more time, take advantage. Go out and see the wonders of the world!

INSTANT ACTION STEP

Take five minutes right now to think about the places you have been.

How did you feel? What was different from where you live?

What did you learn, love or dislike?

What is on your bucket list yet to be visited?

If travel is your passion, what five actions can you do, starting today to make it happen?

SECRET #7

KEEP CONTACT WITH YOUR CHILDREN AND BUILD LONG LASTING-RELATIONSHIPS.

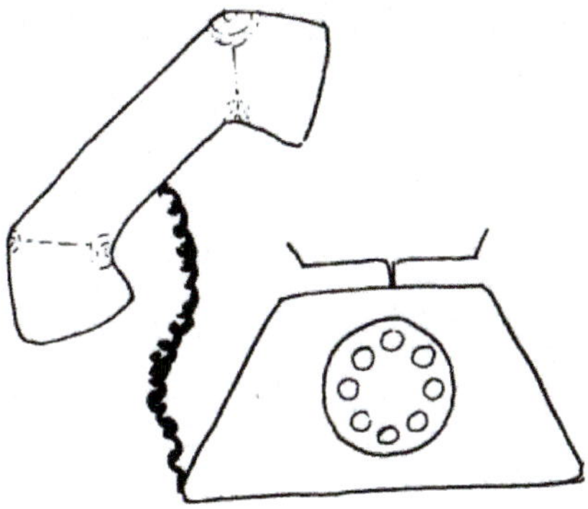

“Success isn't about how much money you make; it's about the difference you make in people's lives."
_Michelle Obama

Your children are gone, but this does not mean the end of your relationship with them. They are out of sight but close to the heart.

We are fortunate nowadays to have all means of communication with the development of mobile phones and the Internet with its related services: WhatsApp, Skype, Snapchat, Teams, Zoom, etc. Google Maps can help you to localize and virtually visit their neighborhood, an action that might seem odd and even stalkerish to some (as my daughter made me realize), but that felt necessary, natural, and comforting for me when they moved to a continent on the other side of the Atlantic Ocean. These options give us at least an illusion of being together even if we cannot kiss or hug.

As a seasoned globe trotter, I see the development of technology as a relief. Technology allows me to continue being connected to my loved ones wherever I travel. In the 1990s, long-distance connections during travel were dependent on phone booths and hotel cell service with exorbitant prices. Later Skype calls required a laptop and Internet cable connection. Today, people can stay connected at 10,000 miles in the sky for virtually no cost. This development is huge and has significantly changed how families as well as corporations and the world communicate.

Your children are out there in the world, gaining experience and growing, maybe close to you or maybe far away. Luckily, the world of IT makes our lives easy, so take advantage and stay connected to your children. Use this opportunity to maintain a strong relationship and to be there when your children need you. Nowadays e-mail, Facebook, video calls and economical airfares have made it convenient for parents to stay in contact with children after they leave home and start independent lives. It has been proven that nowadays parents can stay in touch with their children by calling regularly, texting, emailing and talking with them through video calls. We forget what a revolution it is to see someone on the other side of the world, in real-time, while talking on the phone.

I have noticed that, at the beginning of the separation, the phone calls are frequent and regular, but they lessen with time. You can be in different time zones, but you can always find time to connect. For several years, my family has been spread across three continents: my husband and I (in different countries) in Africa, my girls in Canada, and my boy in South Korea. To manage this situation, I pinned the time zone for each family member to facilitate our staying in touch with one another. Scheduling a weekly or bi-monthly family call helps a lot. While finding a convenient time for everyone may be difficult, I continue to make the effort to make these calls happen.

When I was growing up, a letter could take months to reach its destination, followed by months of waiting for a response. Imagine if you were waiting for an answer to an emergency. I once wrote a letter to my mum—this wonderful woman who raised me and enrolled me in the most prestigious schools. (She is my aunt, and the one I consider my mum.)

I wrote her when she was based in Beijing, China as a diplomat and I was in Burkina Faso. In the letter, I sought her advice about my having been asked to travel to the village with someone with whom I did not feel safe. I had a gut feeling. My mum's response arrived after I returned! I was lucky; I got back safely.

Who writes letters these days? Except for communications between corporations and technical or financial partners, & on holidays or for celebrations, current contact involves email, phone calls, and online meetings.

The Covid pandemic made online communications ubiquitous and part of our daily lives. Consider online meetings with your children and other family members.

You may need to adapt to the different communication needs or wants of your children. Some might want frequent phone calls, while another may only want an occasional call to catch up. My son can "go missing" for a while. He will disconnect all his gadgets and re-emerge when he is ready to reconnect. But when he visits, he is completely with us in a way I can feel. My eldest daughter regularly calls and shares the details of her life. My youngest daughter is unhappy that she always has to call me; I am guilty as charged. Indeed, as parents, we are responsible for keeping the connection, no matter the challenges, by adopting measures to stay connected with our family.

People have different coping mechanisms, but a lot depends on the proximity of the relationship parents and children share.

Never let physical distance become a barrier between you and your loved ones, especially when it concerns your children. If you want a real eye-opener, ask them to describe their feelings about you and their home, but be prepared because you may not like what they have to say. However, their response will help you to better understand them and deal with the barriers that might exist between you. You cannot change something unless you are willing to acknowledge its existence and that sometimes change must begin with you.

As time goes by, your relationship with your child will change as your child grows and develops. To stay close with your children, working on relationship building with them is important. To develop and maintain a strong bond that lasts a lifetime takes great parental effort. Fortunately, if through relationship building you remain available to your children during their teen and young adult years and beyond, your bond will be stronger for their lifetime. Relationships are built through trust, support, and communication.

Communication, the key for building any type of relationship, is especially vital between parents and children. Communication done right forges mutual trust and respect that is essential for a strong and lasting bond.

INSTANT ACTION STEP

Take five minutes right now to reflect on the relationship you have with your children.

Are you happy with the relationship?

What would you improve?

What is dear to you and to them?

What are five actions you can do starting today to build a new long-lasting relationship with your children?

Birguy, giving a speech as president of Leo Club, at Lions Congress, Bingerville, Cote d'Ivoire, 1995

Birguy, attending officials' Lions Club meeting, Ouaga, Burkina Faso, 1995

At Norris Dam, International Leadership Visitors Program, USA- 2003

Birguy, Niger, river basin conference, Cotonou, Benin, 2002

Birguy, UN-Water meeting, Nairobi, Kenya, 2016

The two girls of the "CEE" during a field trip, Lake Tengrela, Banfora, Burkina Faso, 1991.

Gold prospection, High River Gold, Taparko, Burkina Faso, 1996

Working on a pottery wheel- Cuenca, Spain, 2018

Dancing with Colombian dancers, Cartagena, Colombia, 2017

With my husband, at Cuenca, Spain, 2018

My children, Ouaga, Burkina Faso, 2008

With my daughters, Ottawa, Canada 2022

With my children, Zanzibar, Tanzania , 2017

Birguy, Rarotonga, Cook Islands, 2015

Birguy , Hawai,USA, 2017

Birguy , Split, Croatia, 2022

Steering committee members of CEM-IUCN, Costa Rica, 2015

CEM-IUCN members, Pokhara, Nepal, 2018

WHO MISSED WHOM?

Standing alone at the top of the stairs,
She breaks down and cries to her husband,
Daddy, our baby's gone.'
_'She's Leaving Home', John Lennon, Paul McCartney (1967)

Fifty-six years ago, the Beatles sang movingly about what has since been termed the 'Empty Nest Syndrome,' that phenomenon where a parent or parents, having raised children, find themselves bereft when the last child leaves home.

That mothers and fathers are equally affected refutes the claim that mothers, as primary caregivers, are more affected than their male counterparts.
In most cases, both parents are emotionally attached caregivers, although they might be affected differently when the children leave the nest. Some parents may feel a sense of freedom more than sorrow, which allows them to develop a strong bond with their partner and positive relationships with siblings, family and friends in addition to exploring a new purpose and goals in life.

In a study published in 2000, Karen Fingerman[10] interviewed independent women in their twenties and their mothers who were in their forties. Fingerman found that both enjoyed a positive relationship because of the absence of the day-to-day stress caused by living together[11].

10Fingerman, Karen L. "We Had a Nice Little Chat: Age and Generational Differences in Mothers' and Daughters' Descriptions of Enjoyable Visits." The Journals of Gerontology: Series B, Volume 55, Issue 2, 1 March 2000, Pages P95–106. https://doi.org/10.1093/geronb/55.2.P95

11Davis, Eden M.; Kim, Kyungmin; and Fingerman, Karen L. "Is an Empty Nest Best?: Coresidence With Adult Children and Parental Marital Quality Before and After the Great Recession." J Gerontol B Psychol Sci Soc Sci. 2018 Mar; 73(3): 372–381.
Published online 2016 Mar 24. doi: 10.1093/geronb/gbw022

I sent a manuscript of my book to a friend to review, and she gratefully shared poems her mother wrote when she and her brother were leaving the nest. I found them to be an original way not only to say goodbye but to cope with the changes in her life. With her permission, here they are:

WHEN THEY GO TO COLLEGE_

Suddenly
Absence presses like a thorn;
Gathers all the days
Since they were born
Into a constricted swallow;
Makes of their room a hollow
Echoing place
Where trophies on the wall,
Careless books within a stall
Face you with emptiness . . .

Quickly then
Task the hands, the mind;
Sublimate the severance deep within;
Find anodyne in outward thought;
Hold to the fullness
Their years have brought . . .
One must stand firm
Before this sudden lurch
Of loneliness.

SEWING NAME TAGS FOR A SON STARTING COLLEGE_

My needle goes
In and out
And every stitch
Traces the beloved pattern
Of his years.
Now that he
Is about to go
I must not let him know
How sewing name tags
Leaves sharp needle pricks
On my unthimbled heart.

THE LAST ONE GOES TO COLLEGE_

"Goodbye, goodbye…
I'll phone, I' write…."'
(Behind the closed door
Now an empty stillness,)

How like a buoyant breeze she romped along
The flying years, scattering as she rushed,
Her room, disheveled constantly
(records, keepsakes, feminine debri
Now crisply ordered, bleakly stares at me.
Her keenest fun was sew
Into a uniform of green and white.
(I hear the echo of her bouncy cheer
Across a football-charged October night,)
I fold it carefully
For storing in a drawer
And gazing through her bedroom pane
At the gold-red blaze of this September day,
See for a hollow moment but
The lonesome branches of stripped winter trees.

Coping mechanisms are different for different people, but a lot depends on the closeness parents & children share. When children leave their parents, both feel the separation. I started writing this book reflecting on my own reality. Then it occurred to me that I might not be the only one experiencing this situation. I thought it would be good to present views from parents, mums and dads, and also grown children who have also gone through this journey. To gain their perspectives, I conversed with women and men and sent a questionnaire to children.

I posed the following questions and asked them to share one lesson:

Parents:

1. Tell me about yourself.
2. Did you choose to see your children leave the nest? Why? Given the opportunity, would you choose differently?
3. How did you feel? Did you experience empty nest syndrome? How?
4. How did you feel about your children navigating the world alone? Did you worry about their being ready and well-equipped with correct tools? Were you confident you prepared them adequately?
5. How did you cope with the empty nest?
6. Have you one lesson, recommendation, or secret you wish to share with other parents?
7. Have I your permission to share your story in my forthcoming book? I will send you a copy to review and approve before publication.

Grown-up children

1. Tell me about yourself.
2. Did you choose to leave the nest? Why?
3. Would you do it differently?
4. How did you feel about navigating the world alone?
5. Did you feel you were ready? Well-equipped with correct tools?
6. Were you confident your parents adequately prepared you for this experience?
7. How did you cope with the situation?
8. What one lesson, recommendation or secret do you wish to share with other children?
9. Have I your permission to share your story in my forthcoming book?

Enjoy reading their stories that follow.

WHAT OTHER PARENTS SAY

GISELA MARIA MAHLER, MOTHER OF ONE

Lesson 1: "Accept that your child is not there to pursue and fulfill your dreams. Make sure you enable your child to pursue and fulfill his/her own dreams."
_Gisela Mahler

My name is Gisela Mahler. I am German, fifty-eight-years-old, and a single parent. My daughter Hannah is twenty-eight.

I have spent sixteen of my fifty-eight years abroad: one year in England (1983/84), five years in the USA (1988-1993), five years in India (1993-1998), and four plus years in Burkina Faso, West Africa (2000-2004). I studied political science at Universität Konstanz (Germany) and at Rutgers, The State University of New Jersey, USA, and earned a master's degree in 1992.

I was still a graduate student when I got involved in the work of UNIFEM, the UN Development Fund for Women, today called UN Women. Once my studies were accomplished, I was recruited by UNIFEM and sent to India to support the Regional Office in New Delhi in its work for women's development in South and South-East Asia. My last assignment abroad was with the German Development Service (Deutscher Entwicklungsdienst DED) in Burkina Faso, where I supported the women's network RECIF/ONG with my expertise.

We have since returned to Germany and settled in Saarland—a region that was tossed around in history between France and Germany. The corner suited us—my daughter Hannah and me—against all odds. I was able to find a job with international relevance (at first), and Hannah found a French-German school there, which is what she needed at the time.

Since we moved back to Germany in 2004, almost nineteen years have passed. I have moved on job wise, working in the public sector and at the local level with struggling youngsters. Hannah has grown up in the meantime. Having grown up partly in India, Africa, Germany and close to France, and speaking English, French, or German according to requirement, she has turned into a woman with her own perspectives, her own professional path, her own life.

Hannah left her nest at nineteen—too early for my taste. I would have loved it if she could have stayed at home in her nest during her university studies. But I had to accept that she had other plans for herself. Her plans— become a stage performer and dancer—meant that she had to move out of Saarbrücken and into the world. She now lives in Tilburg, Netherlands, and is making a living as a freelance artist, dancer, choreographer, and movement counselor.

Today I am proud of the woman she has become and how well she navigates her life and her professional path. I, in turn, coped with empty nest by keeping professionally busy—and by keeping the nest full. In the first years after Hannah left, I rented her room to foreign students studying in Germany. It was a great experience that kept me in touch with a young and international crowd, and it helped me to stay open-minded and flexible in my habits and attitudes. Of course, I combat empty nest syndrome nowadays by visiting Hannah's new nest at least once a year, and she revisits her old nest at least as much. We keep very close touch and still enjoy each other's company, rare as it has become.

SANDY LOWE, A BUSINESSWOMAN, WIFE AND MOTHER OF FOUR.

Lesson 2: "Be the example. We should raise our children to leave home, that's how nature is. You don't see a male lion staying with the group. He goes and finds his own territory."
_Sandy Lowe

I am Sandy Lowe. I have my own real estate company that I've been running for the last three decades. My husband of thirty-eight years is an agronomist. Together we have raised our four beautiful children. We live in a retirement village in Zimbabwe. My husband and I are Christians and have instilled very high values into our children.

I was born into a working-class family. My dad worked and my mom was a housewife. We had no domestic help, so we learned to pitch in and do everything ourselves. I have tried to raise my four children along the same lines. My older brothers had to serve in the army, so they were comfortable making their own beds, polishing shoes, cooking, living in the African bush, camping, fixing vehicles, undertaking electrical repairs, cooking, sewing, etc. I have made sure all four of my children are comfortable with all manner of chores and what is required to take care of themselves on a daily basis just as I was raised.

Sadly we lost our first-born son tragically when he was twenty-six.
Two of our children chose to go to universities outside the country. The two who remained in Zimbabwe took over a company that my husband started. Together they are involved in successfully growing and expanding that company. Our only daughter, who was the last born, is an established financial analyst living in South Africa.

My husband and I made the choice for our children to leave the nest because we knew we had to send them out of the country to further their education. We would not do it differently given our circumstances. It is good for them to swing and fly, to make their own experience. Of course, it was tough when each of our children left home to either attend university outside the country or move to a different part of the country expanding the business their Dad began. However, there wasn't really empty nest syndrome as we always trained our children to leave home. As soon as they leave, you are on the phone every day. Then phone calls lessen. The natural progression is for your children to leave home, but you worry in the beginning. IT helps a lot.

Prayer was our coping mechanism. My husband and I would pray for them each night before we went to bed. We did our best and had to trust God that we had instilled in each of them the right standards and biblical values to establish them in becoming well-grounded adults in society. "Raise up a child in the way and when they are old, they will not depart from it."

Thankfully as each child left home, others were usually left behind, so we didn't have to go through the empty nest syndrome. Moving to the retirement village was at first daunting, but now I wouldn't have it any other way. It was time in our lives to embrace the next transition. It's so much fun now when we get together for family functions and holidays to reminisce about events and incidents that formed our relationships and cemented our bonds with each other.

CHRISTINE JAMES, A BESTSELLER AUTHOR, WIFE, MOTHER OF FOUR

Lesson 3: Trust the process, release them to fly, walk the path being set for them by allowing God to birth His purpose for our children."
_Christine James

I am Christine James, a wife of forty-three years, a mother of four, and a grandmother of five. I am a lady who comes from a lot of emotional trauma, and I had faith from the beginning. Over the years, I have pastored churches in various states and successfully run multiple businesses. I am now an author of a #1 new release book Faith of a Woman.

I created a successful business in partnership with God that requires three things: Faith for you to live out your God-given call; Alignment for Him to move His vision for your vision; and Action. When you combine your faith with action, the Lord will bless that action and your business will bear fruit.

My husband and I chose the empty nest. There was not a lot of communication in my family growing up, and I promised if I ever got married, that we would have that openness in our marriage and talk about everything concerning decisions for our children or ourselves. We set goals and eventually, becoming an empty nest was one of them.

I quickly realized that my first born was about to go off to college. I felt empty, unsure if he was going to do well going off to another state without us. I fell into a depression because I could no longer protect him and watch over him as I had when he was close. I felt the empty nest when my first born left, despite having his siblings still at home. I was empty inside. He was an awesome son. With his dad being in the military, it was mom who was always there. When he was applying for college, he said wanted to go to the University of North Carolina in Chapel Hill. For me, it was too far away, so I said no.

I just couldn't take it. I went into a depression for almost nine months with his leaving for college. He went to Indianapolis, Indiana to a technology school. At that time, the school was only 1% Black, so being in such a small minority was emotionally difficult for him. Each time he came home, I could tell something inside him was changing.
In fact, the first time he came home, we talked about things that, for the first time in my life, left me feeling helpless. I wouldn't ever be able to support him in the way he needed. I didn't know how to help him when he was far away in Indianapolis and I was in Oklahoma. Each time he would call, I could tell his voice was different.
I wouldn't wish the pain I experienced on anyone. Luckily, the pain was only for that child.

I was happy to let my other children take wings and soar. I have become more mature in the ways of God. Also, three-and-a-half years separated my second and first children, so I had time to deal with the empty nest for the remaining children knowing they eventually would leave, too.

But that first child was hard for me. When you asked me that question the first time, right away I said wow, I remember that because I went through a phase of my life where I've felt so empty and so alone, I guess because I've realized he was the first born and that attachment was finished somehow. I have to let go like the eagles. When they have their babies and it's time for their babies to come out of the nest, they just throw them out there. So I had to really learn to release him to the Lord.

I wasn't worried about my son's not being equipped because we trained our children to trust God in their life and be confident in who they were. It was a blessing for my son to be selected to be in this high standard technical school in a beautiful town; that was God's favor.

However, when we got there, right away, we saw all these people coming from the auditorium. I tell you, I can see my son's face. He was wondering where is my color? You know, right away I could sense it was different. Even though we were military and around all nationalities, I felt like something hit me like ohh, I can't leave him here. I couldn't leave my son there, but we had to. He went through a mode of depression for a couple of weeks. He said it was hard for him because everything was different. I was also scared he had to associate with bad company in this new environment. The worst part was when we left him in his dormitory. I could not handle my tears: we are leaving our first born in Indiana, so far from us!

I had to truly let go and trust what I had built in my children: to commit my life, my children to the Lord. That experience built my faith to another level of trusting God to help me in this phase of my life. The experience was a call for me for more prayer to build myself and to realize only God is able to cover and protect my son and allow him to become the man that He had placed within him.

I felt confident the foundation was laid. Now he was on his own, and it would depend on who he met and what kind of spirits were around him who would influence or be influenced by him. Fortunately, over time, he became stronger. He finished school, God blessed him with an awesome job right out of college, and he's still an awesome son. Now he has a beautiful family.

Immersing myself in prayer was my coping mechanism. In addition, I surrounded myself with like-minded faith people. It is very important to be around people who can encourage you even through you are going through that sadness, that hopelessness. My husband helps me a lot! Yes, I did go through that difficult phase. We were also very active in the church. Church plays a big part in your life when you have children leaving, knowing you have built spiritual values in them and that God will protect them and keep them.

That's all you can do at that point. Pray that God has prepared them such that that they will not disappoint but build in us that happiness and assurance knowing we've done everything, and now it’s paying off.

VINCENT SWEENEY, A MANAGER, HUSBAND, FATHER OF THREE

Lesson 4: "Give your children the confidence to try something rather than focus on the risks and the negatives; support their efforts, even if not financially; don't be the one shutting them down, killing their creativity."
_Vincent Sweeney

I'm a husband, father, engineer, and a manager. I'm someone who is maturing in many ways, even in my old age, including in terms of my spiritual growth and even professionally. I believe that I've become a better person with age, in many ways because I'm more patient and try to view things through the lens of my spirituality rather than just through the material world. But viewing life spiritually is not always possible, so it requires a lot of reminders and constant prayer, and this helps a lot in an 'empty nest'.

I've had a hard time coming to terms with the reality that life doesn't necessarily get easier as you get older.
You make more money, you have less responsibility for your children, etc., but when one challenge is overcome, it seems others replace it and, in some instances, these are even more challenging than the one you were able to overcome. Then you realize those earlier challenges were probably preparing you for the greater challenges ahead.

Part of the empty nest syndrome is the feeling that you're 'going to be free': free of them and you don't have to worry about them and support them, and one or two or three less things to think about. In fact, grown children give you much more to think about including, for example, how they're going to pay their rent. They continue to feel that they can fall back on you in times of need rather than now pushing themselves to fend for themselves. I find my children much more expensive than when they were living with me. I spend more on them now when they should be spending money on me, when they should all be employed and showering me with gifts. Alas, the contrary is true.

My children were all employable, but they've chosen different paths. Only one completed his university degree; the rest did technical certificates. They all in some way or another work in the tourism industry, and, of course, that went ‘to the dogs’ when the country started locking down due to Covid 19.

My eldest son, thirty-three, was out of his regular job and had to find other work to do. Fortunately, his wife works for the government, so she still had her job, but her income was not making ends meet. He's got his job back full time since COVID. He is now planning to buy a house. His wife is working, and they have a son.

The second son, thirty-one, did a technical certificate and moved with his girlfriend to live and work in Canada. They started their own venture that didn’t make any money, so we had to rescue him. We employed him to manage our company while we were out of the country, and he moved into our house. Now he's found a couple of opportunities for investment that we recently invested in, and he's gradually building himself up. He got engaged last year, but they are still living with us. His fiancée is a teacher, so they have a steady income, and they've got some other little sources of income. They help other people with their Airbnb, and they manage properties in addition to mine.

They have multiple sources of income, so, he's now doing all right.

The third son, age twenty-six, also came back home after living and working in Canada. He came up with an idea to invest in a boat that we ended up buying for him. He's been trying to restore it for a couple of years now, so we still have to support him financially. He is the one we were most worried about. He doesn't have any money, and he doesn't have a job. He's the one who actually turned us into empty nesters when he went off to school while we were in Nairobi.

We didn’t expect any of them to stay and live with us. It was always our expectation that they would leave at some point. Either they would move out, or we would move out. We're out of the country, and they live in the house as it doesn't make sense paying rent somewhere else. They were all away at some point, and we didn't know if they would stay away. The first son went away to school and his girlfriend was here in St Lucia. They got engaged while he was in university, so he always planned on coming back to live here and getting married. They lived in our house for a short while when we were away before moving out.

With Covid, we are back from Kingston, Jamaica and working from home, here in St Lucia. We've been here for quite a few months, although we hadn't planned on being here for so long. We ended up living in the same house with my second son. I'll say they tolerate us, and we tolerate them. The arrangement is okay for a temporary situation, but when we finally move back here when I retire, they will have to find their own place. Maybe they can stick around for a little while, but I'm not inviting my children to move back in with me.

I wouldn't do anything different. I know a lot of people who tell their children as soon as they're old enough to move out. That's a North American thing more so than a Caribbean thing. In the Caribbean, people live at home a lot longer. That's probably due to the fact that it's much more expensive to get your own place here. Getting a loan in North America is much easier. Interest rates are lower, etc., whereas down here it's much harder to get your own place. So children typically stay at home a lot longer.

We didn't experience empty nest syndrome at all. We were quite happy to have them gone. It gives us the freedom to do whatever we want whenever we want. We have been so happy being empty nesters, that, right now, we're looking forward to being back in

Kingston where we won't have to deal with other compromises of living with people whose way of doing things is not compatible with our way of doing things.

We gave them enough. I don't think I was worried they couldn't cope on their own. I think they all know how to cook a meal, enough to survive, and they can find information on the Internet. From that point of view, I don't think we were worried. They have a budget and have to learn to live within the budget. Again, they never starved, and they usually found part-time jobs, so at least they were trying to make ends meet. I'll make sure they have some spending money on their own.

Our children have this entrepreneurial mind but it has been a challenge! They were hard-working, so that's one good thing. They are trying, and they try hard. Maybe the ideas were at the wrong time? Or maybe the idea was wrong? But they've tried, and I think they've learned all along. I mean, what's the purpose of working and having income for a rainy day if you're not going to use it on those rainy days? We are fortunate to have all that we need already, so helping them out makes sense.

They learn how to deal with adversity, they learn what does not work, and they remain creative and continue to show initiative. If you shoot down every idea they have with all the negatives, they may either stop having ideas or stop sharing them.

I try to listen more. As far as being objective, I try not to immediately respond with the ‘what ifs’. I listen to them now rather than provide advice—which men generally like to do. We like to solve problems rather than listen. That's one thing I'm trying to do more, and especially with the young men. They want to do things on their own. They want to establish themselves and prove themselves and so on. You have to let them learn and make mistakes, and take some risks. I think it's much harder for mothers than fathers to see their children out on a limb, you know? Whereas it might be exciting to see, and be proud of the limits reached, the mother might be terrified. Why is he going so far out? It's true that men and women look at things very differently.

CELINA RAY, AUTHOR, WIFE, AND MOTHER OF THREE

Lesson 5: "Do your job. Give your children a good foundation. You can never give them enough. You can't equip your children with every tool, right?"
_Celina Ray

I am Celina Ray, forty-eight years old. I was born in Grenada. I came to Canada when I was two years old. My parents first came to Canada for two years to settle themselves before bringing me here.

I started my career late because I had a tough time at undergraduate university where I took six years to finish a three-year degree.

I wanted to be a neurosurgeon, but when I graduated, it was really bad, and I couldn't be a doctor. However, once you pick that you want to be a doctor, that's like your trajectory, right? Unfortunately, getting into university and being the first in my family to go to university didn't work out so well. So I didn't know what I was going to do with the rest of my life. I had to go back to undergrad where I did a research course and ended up loving research. Working in neurological research, I was a research student, followed by a research assistant, then a research coordinator. I fell in love with research, particularly with the niche of brain research. I started my own company, Resolve Research Solutions, Inc., which was a healthcare-based research management company, and again I worked on clinical trials. I was the co-chair of Canada's first national epidemiology study of neurological conditions.

I decided to run for federal politics in Canada. I won the general election and served from 2015 to 2019 with the current Prime Minister, Justin Trudeau, as parliamentary secretary to the prime minister and parliamentary secretary for international development. However, I had a hard time in Canadian politics as the only black female who had been elected out of 338 people, so at the end of my term in 2019, I left the Liberal Party and sat as an independent.

I'm currently doing my PhD in neuroscience, and I am also participating in the Deepak Chopra program to become a certified lifestyle coach—just taking a different sort of journey into a more inward self.

I've been married for twenty-four years. My children are twenty-three, eighteen, and fourteen years old. They've been on this journey the whole time; I've never been alone. I decided they had to go away to school. They could go and come as often as they wanted, but they had to go away.

I made that decision because I felt like I missed the experience of university, that ability to lose some of my naivete about the world. For example, my first daughter has her law degree, and my second child is going into electrical engineering, so they are smart! You know, you can be smart in those areas, but if you can't navigate the world, what is the point?

I made my decision so they wouldn't leave university naive, which I felt I did. I didn't know the ways of the world, so to speak, and so I would not do anything differently. My first daughter went to the University of Leicester to do her law degree and was living in England. We dropped her off and never went back. My second daughter is staying at residence at the University of Toronto even though we live in Toronto.

We have a map in our house like yours (pointing to the map behind), and we put pins on the map where we've all traveled—where we've been in the world. Most of the pins in the map represent my daughters traveling by themselves. They've traveled to more countries than I have. You just give them a good foundation, and you tell them to explore life. You get that understanding when you have a worldly experience.

Before Covid 19, I didn't experience empty nest syndrome. I would have said, when they left, I was fine. I was a little sad, but nothing, really. However, the pandemic was something different. It forced everyone to come back home. At the beginning of the pandemic, my eldest was in England and my middle child was in Australia by herself with a friend of the same age.

Then the prime minister of Canada went on TV and said if you're Canadian and abroad, you need to come home now. I started feeling like what kind of mother just sent her child to Australia, like I had this profound sense of guilt. When they came back home due to the pandemic, I realized how much I'd missed them. I got an opportunity to do things differently. So whereas before I took for granted things like having dinner together, now we always have dinner together at night. We always do so many things together now.

But during the pandemic, I loved it and realized how much I missed the togetherness. The time together because of the pandemic just made me realize that their being home is fantastic.

I feel terrific seeing my children navigating the world alone. I've raised these children that way; even my son traveled alone when he was only five or six years old. We just put him on a plane to go and visit his grandparents in Florida. I feel really like I've given my children the foundation they need to be able to navigate the world. Even in a peculiar precarious situation, like Covid 19, they were still able to navigate the world.

When the instruction was given to bring all Canadians back home, I got my fifteen-year-old-daughter back first from Australia. My eldest followed. She still had an apartment in England where her boyfriend lived, and she'd been finishing school, but she had to do a couple of exams. She could have done the exams here, but she could have stayed and done the exam there, too. I was not sure she would agree to come home, but she came. This really made me understand the power of building that foundation: even though she had all of these things she wanted, the need to be home during this crisis superseded her own selfish endeavors. I felt that guilt for a little while, and then I just recognized I'd raised some good children.

You can never give your children enough. You can't equip them with every tool, right? So even when they were going to the park around the corner or going to the mall to hang out with their friends, I would say to them: “If you want this to be the last time you go, make it happen.” In that statement they knew they should not steal from the mall; they shouldn't act the fool in the mall; they shouldn’t do anything they knew they shouldn't do. I didn’t have to go through the whole list. But if they wanted this to be the last time they went to the mall alone, they could make that choice. If they wanted this to be the last time they went to the park, they could make that choice. So it made them think: Do I trust my gut when my gut is telling me something is going wrong and it’s not on my mom’s list? It's not on the list because I didn't give them a list of good or wrong, right? I gave them a foundation that they've had since birth of how to conduct themselves at the park or at the mall or in a foreign country. So while I'm never sure if I've given them the correct tools, I’m confident I gave them a good foundation. Whether you lose trust or not is your responsibility, not mine. I've done my job. Now it's your job to take what I've given you and use it wisely, and I'm confident you can do that.

I guess this is where, as a parent, you know what sort of parameters to put in place, all those extra above and beyond on safety precautions—making sure, of course, that they have money, that all their papers are current, and also ensuring that global affairs knows they're traveling.—. So even when my children were in Australia and England, we were conversing. We were outside of the country, and what was the timeline for my getting them back home? When were the flights going to stop? How could they be extradited from those foreign places and brought back here? As an adult, I needed to do the things that I know my children didn't have the experience to think of. For example, even though she was reluctant, I had to fly my daughter in Brisbane to Sydney where it was easier to get a flight out of Sydney. Many times, I had to step in calmly. I wasn't doing anything at the last minute, even in the fluid situation of a pandemic, everything was well thought out. I had to be twenty-five steps ahead of where they currently were and have contingency plans in place. For example, I advised my daughter to contact a storage company before coming back to Canada so moving wasn't a panicked situation, even if something went awry. My priority was to make sure they were safe.

I have my job, my house to look after, bills to pay, and then I have to worry about foreign countries' policies. I was constantly looking at Google maps and Snapchat or trying to geolocate my children, and looking at what was happening in foreign jurisdictions where they were. The situation added a layer of stress I didn’t appreciate until they were home. I can turn off the TV and not watch the news because they're right here. Now I could breathe that sigh of relief. I could relax a little bit. As much as we want them to leave and experience the world, tension is associated because your job as a parent is to keep them safe, which adds to everything else you do in your daily life. At least, when your children are around, you have peace of mind and can focus on other things.

I have this mantra that I live by. It's just a way of being, I guess. I say to my mom and my children—anybody who knows me—that when I die, I want it to say on my tombstone: All she had left to do was die. To live, to experience life, to do everything so that at the end, they're like oh, man—meaning she's done everything. I want the same for my children. They can't live if we are holding them and setting our arbitrary boundaries regarding what they can do or writing a list of things they can't do and not saying it's your responsibility. We can't set up real or arbitrary boundaries and expect our children to live. I want them, when they are going through life, to just say yeah, what is this opportunity? Where is it? Burkina Faso?. Yeah. Let's go. Let's do that. Let's see how that works. And if it works, great. If it doesn't work, great. It doesn't matter.

Does whether something works out matter in living and in experiencing your spirit in the world? Does it matter if it works or it doesn't work? No. Just live while you're alive. The destination never matters. It's in the moments along the journey that you are experiencing life, the ones where you stop and smell the roses. That’s what matters.

SAFIA BARRY, INTERPRETER, WIFE, AND MOTHER OF THREE

Lesson 6: "You must stay very close to your children even when they leave the family nest."
_Safia Barry[12]

I grew up in a polygamous family. The compound was always full of people: my brothers, my sisters, and all the children my father hosted at his house. At one point, fourteen children were in the compound. When I got my CEPE (Certificate of Primary Elementary Studies) and entered the sixth grade, I was sent to Koudougou. At that time, the best were chosen to be

[12] This wonderful woman left us on June 25th, just before this book is published. May she RIP

sent to the best schools, which were boarding schools run by nuns. I left the family nest at the age of eleven. It was the first time I left my parents. My older brother Abdourahmane (now a professor), who was at university, accompanied me to college where I boarded.

When I succeeded to the BEPC (Bevet d'Ếtudes du Premier Cycle du Second Degrế/Certificate of Studies of the First Cycle of the Second Degree) and the entry in second, I was directed to the College Notre Dame de Kologh-Naba. However, I lived far away and had no means of transportation. so I asked to be transferred to Zinda high school until the BAC (baccalaureate). I then went to the University of Ouagadougou to do a master's degree in English language. I always dreamed of doing translation. I enrolled in the USA, but when I got there, the cost of living was too expensive. I had to pay a deposit or get a job, neither of which I had, so my travel to the USA turned out to just be a vacation, as I had to go back. Instead, I went to Cameroon to train and returned in 1992. I worked for UNICEF for two years until they offered me a job that was not my profile, so I stopped and started my own business. By the grace of God, I am doing well.

I am married and have three children.
My husband and I have always wished that the children could study in the best schools. My oldest son graduated from high school at seventeen and wanted to be an engineer. He enrolled in Moncton, Canada. That trip was the first time he traveled alone. I wanted to request a visa to go with him, but his father said to let him fend for himself, and that's what he did. He found summer work early on and took care of himself while in school. He even managed to afford his own car.

Our second daughter chose foreign relations and political diplomacy. She was less disoriented because she had her uncle in France where she stayed until she found her apartment. She also found a job very early and took care of herself. The last baby is about to leave this year and the nest will be really empty.
When the children left, I felt a little lonely. I couldn't wait for their vacations to come so they could return. I see their rooms closed and feel sad. it's true that social networks have helped us a lot: we make video calls and have family meetings using WhatsApp, so everyone sees each other and talks. The work I do has also helped ease the loneliness: when I start to think a lot, an upcoming trip takes my time and allows me to forget. What I really miss is having them all home at the same time!

I think we have given our children basic values. They also surprised me a lot by how quickly they adapted, found a job, and even took care of themselves during their studies. I know of families where the children have not been able to adapt to the studies or to the harsh climate of Canada. My children have had tough experiences, but each time we talked, they were motivated to finish what they left for. I tell them when they're done, they can come home. While they're away and I prepare a meal they like, I think of them and say aloud, "I hope they have eaten well, too." I don't know what they ate that day, but as I am always between two planes, I feel less empty.

When I left the family nest, we had no phone, or WhatsApp to communicate easily. To get an answer from letters could take months. You have to stay very close to your children even when they leave the family nest. If they stay away for a few days, you should always call them to see if everything is going well. You have to be in touch every day.

CHRISTOPHER COX AND TANYA MATHEW–COX, PARENTS OF THREE

Lesson 7: 'The thing is, in life expect that there will be changes; things don't stay as they are… Children grow up and you have to be prepared to let them do their own thing. Let them be their own person, and give them the opportunities to experience life on their own.' _Chris Cox

I could be considered an environmental spirit, but somebody who sees the environment through art. I guess my calling in life and career has been to see and inspire others to see beauty in nature, which has been central to what I have been doing. From my teenage years though my professional career, art has been a part of my personality. This is how I define myself. I was born in Toronto, Canada, but grew up from a very young age in Saint Lucia, a small island in the Eastern Caribbean, which is home for me and my family. I now work overseas, but my mom and sister live in Saint Lucia, and my brother lives in Canada.

On joining the United Nations Environment Programme (UNEP) near the end of 2014, I moved to Nairobi, Kenya and was joined by my wife and the last two children by the middle of 2015. We had a great experience in Kenya. For me, it was a welcome opportunity given my desire to experience the 'world', perhaps more widely than what I was exposed to having grown up and lived on a small island, even though I cherished the relaxed island life. Tanya shared this vision and desire, so it drove our decision to gain other life experiences and, of course, the career opportunities working for the United Nations opened up. Our time spent in Kenya was an enriching experience both from a work and social standpoint. In mid-2019, I took another position within UNEP, this time at the duty station in Panama City, Panamá—his time in an entirely Spanish-speaking environment. These experiences have no doubt shaped our life-outlook, reflect on who we are, on our mission, which would have perhaps been different had we remained in Saint Lucia.

We have three children: sons Aidan and Jason, ages 29 and 24, and a daughter Layla, age 19.

When we moved from Saint Lucia to Kenya, Aidan was already at university in Canada, so, he didn't live with us in Nairobi although he came to visit. Jason graduated from high school in Kenya after two years. Layla remained with us and moved with us to Panamá in 2019. Layla graduated from high school in Panamá in 2021, so the nest is now empty except for our lovable dog Joey who has been part of the family since Kenya. We were equally resigned to the empty nest choice. That they would leave the nest was a foregone conclusion as we always imagined they would go off from an early age and live their own lives, first to pursue higher education at university, and after, the world! We wouldn't have done it any differently necessarily.

We first felt that odd empty nester sensation when the eldest left to go to university while we were still living in Saint Lucia. It was a feeling of loneliness as someone in your circle with whom you interact on a daily basis is not around. His voice is not in the room, I'm not seeing him…he's so far away. You are left with a sense of something missing; this place just doesn't feel the same. Not only did Tanya and I feel it, so did the younger children. They were without the anchor and sharp-witted humor of big brother! However, as parents, I think the feeling of separation was a bit different with me compared to Tanya.

Tanya has been very involved in levels of detail during the 'fledging process': setting them up at university, checking to see how they're managing in navigating the new life, helping with tasks, giving advice, and actively assisting where needed—sometimes with me objecting: "Let them learn!" Tanya was still getting involved in all their activities as she would have done if they were physically with us. She has that kind of drive to make sure that she keeps in touch with everything; well, she is a mom! I'm more hands off. That's the difference. Notwithstanding, for both of us, there's a feeling of emptiness, more so that all three children are now out of the house.

At first, we were a bit concerned about seeing our children navigating the world alone. In the initial year of university, all three went through similar feelings of uneasiness. It took time to settle in, much having to do with cultural differences.

For example, Aidan, who pursued a journalism degree, found it hard to appreciate the cultural and historical contexts in Canadian-based curricula content compared to his mostly Canadian peers. This impacted his initial confidence and how he related to his peers. His experience reminded me of my own when I went off to university as an island boy of mixed race in a very culturally different northern rural Canadian small town.

We were there for Aidan, encouraging him to get on, and soon he got into a groove.

With Jason, who also studied in Canada, the process was relatively smooth, although he had initial apprehension on first leaving and being on his own. But he was in the same town with Tanya's relatives, and, Aidan, after graduation, landed a job in the same town where Jason was studying, so that helped.

Layla is also now in Canada but in a different city doing her studies. What is nice is that there is a sizable Caribbean student community among whom she can share 'familiar' Caribbean experiences. She also went through some separation anxiety, maybe because, as the last in the family and as the girl, we held her more closely? Certainly, in the pandemic years we were shuttered in Panama, so maybe we are partly responsible for her initial trepidation. Anyway, she is doing quite well now!

I think we were able to give them the survival tools they need. Children growing up are exposed to all types of influences, both positive and negative, and the late teen years is when they are defining their personalities, their orientations, and, with the transition out of the home, it is crucial that they are oriented in the right way. Our children have been able to fit within the environments they have found themselves in. They have found their way and have been able to adapt well—at least, until now we haven't seen anything to suggest otherwise, for which we are thankful! Sometimes I (we) do wonder whether we gave them enough, but this will always be an open question. I think laying down a good foundation is the most important part. Now our role is just making sure we can support them every now and then as needed, for example, when something may be weighing on their minds, we have to make sure we are there for them.

Now that it's just Tanya and me, we find that sometimes there's like open space between us. We are still in a three-bedroom house.
We often have long quiet times not having children around anymore, where I am normally outside working from the terrace (in the COVID-time home office), while Tanya is working inside on her online business. We have dinner together, of course, and watch TV after, & sometimes on weekends go out somewhere. Certainly, it's not like before when the children' lives spun our lives and social relationships, particularly as an expat family living in a foreign country. With the children around, there would often be social get-togethers among parents, but this doesn't happen

anymore. During the COVID pandemic we were isolated in Panamá for practically two years, and Layla's leaving for school in the fall of 2021 seems to have magnified this feeling of change. We are still in that kind of mood, but we're gradually emerging from it. I think for all parents, transitions with children leaving home during the COVID pandemic isolation period have yielded experiences that we may not have had if we had not had the pandemic, but who knows?

I remain busy at work, and Tanya works on her online business, creating print-on-demand merchandise inspired by her experiences when we were still living in St Lucia where she was promoting and marketing my artwork on a range of merchandise items.
She also at the time created her own product line. The difference now is that she has taken that business online. In addition, we've converted our house in Saint Lucia to an Airbnb property, and that takes up management time on her part.
While we have a property manager in St. Lucia, Tanya is always in contact with respect to maintenance work and handling bookings. That aspect is the kind of thing I don't like to do, which I'm thankful for because I know for me it would just be a headache!

The key thing is not to overshadow your children much, or they become dependent on you.

They will not consider their identity as their own, but something that's defined by their parents. Allow them to experience situations in which they have to think on their own, interact with people beyond their immediate family, and circle as key to building their own resilience and discovery. The experience of leaving home today is different from our days, reflecting thirty years ago. Back then when you left home for university, there was no social media to keep in close contact with family and friends, albeit digitally. So, when you left, you really 'left'. Being apart really meant being on your own without your familiar support network, so you had to figure things out on your own. Granted, we have moved on with the times, but the basics remain the same: encourage your children to be who they are; give them space to grow; provide the foundation for them to do so; and know that you will have to let go for them to carve their own path! And keep cheering!!!

LYDIA EIBL-KAMOLLEH, RETIRED, MOTHER OF THREE

Lesson 8: 'As I was a single parent, I wish we could have been two parents because nature has planned it that way and for a reason'
_Lydia Eibl-Kamolleh

I am sixty-five years old. I retired in March 2022. I am German by nationality, and I reside in Kenya where I have lived for over thirty years.
Kenya is my home and, for my three children (Marc-Jamal, thirty-five; Nadine-Raissa, thirty-two; and Noor-Adrian, thirty-two) who were all born here in Kenya, this is home. My Kenyan husband, from whom I got divorced in 2000, unfortunately passed away in December 2018.

I worked in Kenya for the private sector as a financial controller, was a consultant for water management and PPP (Private Sector Participation), and for the last nineteen years worked for the UN as a fund management officer.

My children went to the German School, then left the nest because university was only feasible abroad. That choice was made by my children. They looked forward to going abroad, and I agreed. I still believe that was the right decision because our responsibility as parents is to guide and prepare them for life out there and for them to be stable on their feet. Exposure and education are key, hence, yes, I would do the same or better support their decision again.

I did not have empty nest syndrome. I worked for financial reasons before I had my children and throughout the time they were under my care. I had no alternative. When they were ready to go and excited about it, I was ready as well.

My children were traveling from the age of five as 'unaccompanied minors'. They spent their holidays in Germany with my parents. I joined at the end, and we traveled back to Kenya together. They loved it. I could see that from an early age, they were more independent than others.

I felt that exposure was to their benefit. At an early age, I had to leave them in childcare. In Kenya this was possible, and I had no alternative anyway. We optimized the time I/we had with them, and I often felt that I spent more quality time with my children than mothers who were at home looking after their children as their full-time occupation. And those children who were then eighteen years old navigated the world alone very well. I was confident I gave them enough because I believe I tried my best.

At the same time, I had three young adults abroad at the university while I worked full time, took care of a sick mother, and was frequently on mission. My children understood my situation as a single parent and went through crazy times but came home twice a year. I believe had I been a full-time mother, that time would have been much more difficult, but I always felt that my responsibility was to make my children responsible and independent and able to fit in in this world, which, being racially mixed, was not easy for them.

AMANDA KHOZI MUKWASHI, MOTHER OF TWO

Lesson 9: 'Keeping communication channels open helps to mature together'.
_Amanda Khozi Mukwashi

I am a married mother of two adult children. They left of their own choice. They were probably looking for their own independence. We missed their presence in the house. We missed their laughter and just knowing they were there. However, it also feels good that they are able to live on their own and find their own path. My children are still navigating the space. It's a lifelong journey. Sometimes you worry about the challenges and other issues that they have to face as they navigate the spaces. You worry about their progress, about their life partners, and just other daily things. Then you realize that there is only so much that you can do to protect them. They have to make their own way in life. It's hard to let go.

I don't think you are ever fully confident that you have done all you can. You simply hope that you have instilled the right values, attitudes, and ethics in them. They have to make their own choices. Being there for them when things work out, you celebrate with them, and when things don't work out, you are a shoulder for them. Sometimes you want to take that pain away, but it is not possible. So you are in a continuous journey of learning and relearning. When you learn new tools, you also share with them. You grow together in love and respect. Keeping communication channels open helps you to mature together.

I cope with the situation by talking. Even when you don't like what you are hearing, it is better when you are all free to express your thoughts about what's happening in your life and how you are feeling. It has taken a while, but we are getting there. As they learn to trust that we respect them as adults, they open up more, and we can therefore support each other.
Prayer has helped me. Prayer continues to be my go-to before, during, and after.

When I don't know; when I have no answers; when I am hurting, and when they are hurting; prayer is my channel for communicating with God for all their and my needs.

COLONEL-MAJOR ABDOULAYE DIALLO AND MRS. HULDA DIALLO DELMA

Lesson 10: "Establish and maintain a communication system when the children are small and even when they leave. It's the basis of everything. And then being present, and listening."
_Abdoulaye Diallo and Mrs. Hulda Diallo Delma

I was born into a polygamous family. My father had two wives. From my mother, I am the only boy. A girl unfortunately died. My second mother has two girls. As far as my schooling is concerned, I came from the Prytanée militaire.
I went to the Military Academy in Madagascar. Then, I started my career as an officer.

I was able to climb all the ranks until I became colonel major on January 1st, 2016.
In addition to my military training, I studied economics at the University of Ouaga, computer science at the CNAM in Paris (National Conservatory of Arts and Crafts, and engineering school), at the Faculty of Science of the University of Bordeaux I, and at the Ecole Supérieure de l'Electronique et de l'Informatique in Bordeaux. I am a network and computer security engineer. I also have a master's degree in computer science applied to business management & a master's degree in mediation and conflict management.

I have held several positions in the Army, including Brigade Commander for the qualification of non-commissioned officers, Chief of Staff of the Commander-in-Chief of the High Command, Chief of the Personnel Division and Chief of the Forward Studies Division of the General Staff of the Army. I was also Defense Attaché at the Embassy of Burkina Faso in Riyadh, Saudi Arabia. Today, I am the Secretary General of the Ministry of Defense and Veterans. At the civilian level, I was Director General of the National Identification Office. I have received five decorations from my country; the most important is the Commander of the Order of the Stallion.

I have been married to Mrs. Hulda Diallo Delma for twenty-five years. We have three lovely children, two boys and a girl. My wife trained as an executive secretary, and she also has a DESS in micro-business management. She has worked in airlines, a law firm, project ‘code of persons and family’, in an international oil company, and in a private firm that assists companies in their various needs such as organization, audit, search for financing. When we were stationed in Saudi Arabia, she worked as a consultant. At the moment, she is the Deputy General Manager in charge of Finance and Accounting in a holding company in Abidjan.

Regarding the children and education, it must be said that the choice to let the children go abroad for their studies was imposed on us. Our first son was in a university in Ouagadougou, so we had the chance to see him every night. Then I was assigned to Saudi Arabia. When we left, he was doing his bachelor's degree, so we left without him. After graduation, he went to France to do a master’s degree. He found a job there.

Our daughter was in her last year of high school when I was going to Saudi Arabia.Even though my mother was watching, I worried my daughter would break down. She said to me: "Dad, don't worry,

I'll pass with honors." I told her: "My daughter, if you pass your baccalaureate with honors, I will enroll you in the university and the country of your choice." She passed her baccalaureate with an average of more than 17, including 19 in math and 20 in physics. However, she could not enter the university system in Saudi Arabia because the courses were in Arabic or English. The training she chose was not available in Burkina Faso, either. So she went to Canada for a difficult course of study, but she did well and obtained her bachelor's degree.

Our youngest son stayed with us in Riyadh and attended the French school where he graduated with honors this year. We had promised to enroll him in the school of his choice. As we were returning to the country and he had the opportunity to have been selected in the
'parcours Sup'[13] system in the best schools, he made his choice for a renowned business school. We honored our promise, which implied letting him go away from us. We also raised my little sister's daughter who is also currently in Canada for a PhD.
Initially, when our children were very small, we agreed that we would not let them go away immediately after

[13] a Web portal designed by the French that manages the balance between undergraduate places in French higher education institutions with the applications of candidates with a high school diploma.

graduation. We have known many children who are out and about who have gone astray. We wanted them to have a bit of a wall, a circle of friends, because it encourages them to come back home after school. However, with their opportunities and our departure abroad, we did not have much choice. We really don't regret our choice because we had a lot of satisfaction. We are lucky to have conscientious children. Early on, they became aware of how life is, how they should behave and take responsibility.

We felt bad when they left. In 2008, we gathered the whole family (the children, including my mom) for the vacations in Riyadh. After that, they started leaving one by one: first my niece, then our first son, then our daughter.

I must admit that every time we accompanied the children to the airport and came back home, it was terrible. Suddenly, the house is not the same. We often want to go and see what is going on in the child's room, and the emptiness is unbearable.

At first, we huddled around the little one who remained. He was our everything. For me, he was really my little friend, the one with whom I played sports. We were close, and most of all, we tease a lot in the family. So, when he left, there was a big void, and the pain became more pronounced:

it was the ultimate. I started to say it's not fair. The school took my children away from me. For a long time, I would get up every morning and open the door to his room to see if he was really gone. I couldn't accept the fact. Although we had accompanied him to the airport, we came back, we slept—the next day, for me, of course he was there. We really had a hard time, but it must be said that nowadays with the new technologies, we communicate regularly, and it relieves us a little. We try to connect with all the children on a regular basis. Their mother especially is much more in contact than I am.

The departure was painful. Already, we had to leave the eldest in Ouaga. He had a health problem, so when he left, it was still difficult, and we were worried. How would he manage on his own? It was stressful and painful. But since we have family in Ouaga, we were more or less reassured. For our daughter, too, we separated with a lot of apprehension. She was very young, seventeen years old, and she had to go so far to Canada by herself, having refused that we accompany her although it was the first time she was traveling alone, so it was not easy. For the last one, as he was the only one who was with us, his departure left a big void because we still had habits, routines, like going to check in his room at night to see if everything was fine, and then waking him up in the morning, doing programs together. On both sides, the departures created a certain imbalance.

Their mother suffered much more than I did because I was always traveling. I was traveling so much that one day, the children said to me: "Dad, now it's over. If you leave for more than a week now, it will be with the family."
An ultimatum! For the little anecdote, my daughter was born behind me, when I was in Bordeaux. The family came to Bordeaux two months later, but as she was very small, she didn't remember. Every time I came on vacation to Ouaga, the little one fled the room. When she needed her mother, she stayed at the door and said: "Mother, I want you." When I came back for good, it was difficult to win back my daughter. I suffered, frankly, and still now this complicity between a father and his daughter is not at the top.

My absence marked me. I realize there are times when you have to be there. I left for four years in Bordeaux, then for a year and a half in Congo. When you travel, no matter how careful you are, no matter how much you leave behind, it is not enough. Indeed, I once shed tears the time my daughter and her brothers stayed with one of her aunts when their mother was on medical evacuation in Paris and I was on mission.

When I called and asked my daughter if they were missing anything, she said, "No, we're just missing you." At that moment, I understood the extent of our absence and the impact on our children.

It is important, even when the children are gone, to continue to be present for them, to give them advice, to listen to them, and to have regular communication with them. When there is a problem, we can solve it quickly and it's a relief. Today, we are lucky to have the technology to communicate quickly and well. We are also lucky to have mobility. They have been able to come for their vacations and leave. The third point is that leaving is a normal stage of life. We, too, had to leave our parents at a certain time. So it's a normal process that we have to accept. Fourthly, we put everything in prayer. It is God who keeps, whether our children are with us or elsewhere, and that calms us.

We were not too worried about our children being alone abroad because we taught them to be responsible and instilled in them a number of values such as not to lie, not to steal, to respect others, etc. We also taught our children from a young age four words: thank you, sorry, excuse me and please. These are lessons that have become automatic. They pay off a lot.

We don't have behavioral problems with our children. We think we have given them the necessary tools: honesty, respect, politeness, hard work,
good resource management. In life, as long as you are polite to everyone, as long as you don't seek harm from anyone, as long as you stay away from evil and fear God, I think you can navigate anywhere in the world.

It is true that we are always worried as parents because we know that in these societies there is not much humanism, but we told ourselves that they can always manage by our giving them the right basics. We really encouraged communication. There are no taboo subjects in the family. The children could talk about anything with us. Also, before leaving they had an overview. They knew how to behave when faced with difficulty. They knew who to talk to because we made them understand that it's only the family that really matters. Even if we are far away, we are always available to listen to them. This is reassuring for them and for us as well. Also, at home, there was no difference in tasks: girl-boy. They all did the cleaning, the tidying up, and some cooking. It was difficult for those who didn't want to do it at all, but we forced it. They told me that I was too complicated, but in the end, at least they all knew how to prepare food and not starve.

When they were leaving, we told each other we had done all that we should and could have, and we made them understand that we were still here, too. We can't claim to have everything covered, but we are always available. It must be said that our children are very modest. They are not envious. They have learned to be content with what they have. We gave them pocket money from a young age, and they learned to manage well. In fact, they have to justify the money they receive this month in order to receive the next. For the record, the youngest child saved his pocket money and sometimes helped me out with interest! The fact that we had family meetings where we explained the merits of a certain number of things formed them and taught them to be responsible and aware.

For example, our daughter managed her money well once in Canada. She was aware that her education was expensive, so when she finished her degree, she decided to work to save money to pay for her master's degree. She knows that we can pay for her education, but she prefers that we focus on her little brother. She even sent us her first paycheck so we could give her blessings, and that really touched us. After our last one left, too, in the morning when we woke up, his mom and I each found an email he'd made thanking us in appreciation for the education he received. He said he recognized that I was often hard, but he understood later that it was only love. A real tribute! This shows that he is a very conscientious child. We are close to our children; they are like our friends. On weekends, we sometimes went outside of Ouaga with the children, and they loved it. We often went on vacation with the children and offered them little pleasures when they needed them. We are happy today to see that the children are very close to each other. They are also caring and never forget our birthdays or wedding anniversary. I remember that on my birthday, when I arrived in Riyadh and as the family was still in Ouaga, they compiled all the pictures of the little outings, the nice moments, and made a little movie to send me., That really touched me.

No matter how busy the parents are, the children need their presence. Money does not replace the presence of parents. You have to be close to the children: talk to them a lot, be attentive to their education and to their attendance. Providing them with the best possible training is also important. Often a source of conflict, the idea of leaving a legacy to a child who has not learned to manage will not serve him much. It's better to invest in giving them the best education and training. That's really what I can recommend.

Today, our children understand all the decisions we used to make that they thought were hard.

We always told them: “You know, parents are never going to intentionally mislead you because they can't mean you harm.” We are open with them, their mom more than I, I have to say.
There's also professional deformation. I'm in the military, & I admit that sometimes I’m bossy. Although I try not to bring the army home, I often say no, and it is definitive, especially in relation to a number of values. So they don't insist. Their mother is also strict, but she has a softer way of getting the message across.

When they are away, we are not physically present, but, through communication and social networks, they know that at any moment they can count on us. They can talk, they can say everything without being judged. We have often said to the children: “You have to say everything, even if I get angry at you right away. In any case, at least I have heard, and we will find a solution together.” The second point is to trust them because they need to feel that trust. If we don't trust them, we suspect them of everything, and they will go and fall where we fear.

Establish a good communication system, be present, and then trust them. I remember our first son, when he was little and I told him not to do something, he would always ask me why.

We have to explain to him, but when he understands the reasoning, when he is convinced, it is forever. When children are afraid of parents, they play at being correct in front of them, but behind them they cheat. It is necessary to establish trust, communication, dialogue, and to be available. Thus, everything becomes easy.

FEEDBACK FROM CHILDREN WHO LEFT THE NEST.

For the children getting ready to explore a new home, perhaps a new country, the prospect of adventure, freedom, and homesickness compete.

Some have waited so long they are eager to deploy their wings. They feel the excitement of escaping high school and parental rules and moving into college dorms or apartments with friends. Other children leave the nest reluctantly, feeling the anxiety of moving out of the comfort zone of home and family. Either way, saying goodbye is not easy, and jumping into the unknown, even though exciting, can be scary.

Here is what some children who flew the nest have to share:

FAIZA CONGO, BANKER, TWENTY-NINE YEARS OLD

Lesson 11: "To any kid leaving to go abroad, I would say, when you move to a new country, be open to learning and discovering."
_Faiza Congo

My name is Faiza Congo. I live in Quebec City where I work as a banker for Scotiabank. I'm from Burkina Faso. I moved to Canada in 2012. My family made the decision for me. Having said that, I didn't want to go to university in Burkina, so I was okay with their decision to send me to Canada. I was relieved to leave the nest and excited to live in a new country. I didn't feel sad or anxious to leave. Funnily enough, the feelings of sadness and nostalgia came years later.

I was excited to be able to navigate the world alone, not worried at all.

Even though I thought I was ready, I clearly wasn't. I was too young and not mature enough to know that I wasn't ready. I wasn't confident my parents had given me the tools to handle things successfully, but I thought I had the tools within me to succeed on this new journey. Again, I was wrong. You live, you learn—that's what happened. I made mistakes; I've learnt from them. I tried to not repeat the same mistakes as I worked to become a better version of myself.
To any kid leaving to go abroad, I would say, when you move to a new country, be open to learning and discovering. The world is big, and there's so much beauty to see! This is a unique opportunity to explore new things and learn what the other culture has to offer. Don't be shy; talk to people. Make (good) friends, study hard, and fall in love when the time is right.

AURELIE CHAPON, ENGINEER, TWENTY-EIGHT YEARS OLD

Lesson 12: "Focus on why you left your comfort zone and your parent's nest, and do not derail from your goal!"
_Aurelie Chapon

I am Aurelie Chapon. I am a dual citizenship of France and Burkina Faso. I was raised through high school in Burkina Faso, more precisely in Ouagadougou, before exploring another country, Canada. I arrived in Montreal in 2012 to pursue my undergraduate studies in Civil Engineering, and I have worked in project management for five years. I recently got my Canadian permanent resident status.

I can say that I actually have my foot on three continents: Africa, Europe, and North America.

I was the one who chose to leave the nest. I have always been interested in discovering new cultures and pursuing my studies in an environment different from my own. I wanted to face the real challenge of life when my parents were far from me and how I could deal with that. Before immigrating to Canada, I was anxious because it was the first time leaving my parents. But as my childhood friends came to Montreal for their studies, I was reassured.

I did not feel ready, but my father came with me to help me set up in Montreal and find an apartment. His support helped me feel less overwhelmed and able to prioritize and organize things. When my father left Montreal, I started finding my way around. I quickly understood how it works here in Montreal in terms of administrative things and the culture in general.

KOLENE LAMIZANA, STUDENT—COGNITIVE SCIENCE AND COMPUTATION, TWENTY-ONE

Lesson 13: "Ask questions, don't buckle up on things that you can get advice on. Always try to find someone, a reliable source to seek for guidance"
_Kolene Lamizana

I am a twenty-one-year-old student. I study cognitive science and computation in Ottawa, Canada. I lived in Burkina Faso my entire early childhood, until I was ten when I moved to Kenya with my mom and brother.
I actually left twice two different nests: first, I left Burkina Faso, where I lived with my dad, to follow my mom with whom I had not lived with for a couple years, and then I left Kenya at sixteen to go to Canada and finish high school.

When I left Burkina Faso, I did not really understand how big of a choice I was making. I was excited to go live in another country with my mom and my brother, but I did not have any big introspective thoughts about what it meant for me and my dad and the family's dynamic. When I left to go to Canada, I knew it was on a whim, and, although I was sad to end a chapter of my life in a country where I spent my teenagerhood and to leave my mom behind, I convinced myself I needed a change of scenery for my growth and well-being.

It's hard to navigate the world alone. It takes time to adjust, to understand the price and consequences of actions and choices, to set healthy habits now that you are responsible for yourself. At first, I felt ready; that's why I left. But with time, you realize all that goes into living an active life where you are responsible for yourself, and it's easy to feel overwhelmed and inept. I did not think about what tools I had, or I'd missed. The experience is something so new that you don't know what you need before actually needing it.

My parents always encouraged me to ask questions when I didn't know, and so I often did to navigate the beginning of my adult life. I also acknowledge the huge privilege I had to have my sister in the same country whom I could turn to, to ask my many questions and learn from her experience.

One recommendation I can give to any kid leaving the nest is: if you're in a healthy environment, enjoy it as long as you can.
There is no rush to leave. Once the nest starts to disperse, it is hard to get that atmosphere back, especially when, like our family, everyone lives far apart. Ask questions. Don’t buckle up on things that you can get advice on. Always try to find someone, a reliable source from whom to seek guidance when it comes to actions you need to take but for which you don’t feel you have the proper knowledge.

KEITH LAMIZANA, MASTER'S DEGREE IN BUSINESS, ENTREPRENEUR, TWENTY-FIVE YEARS,

Lesson 14: "When you leave your nest to go in a new place, find someone who walked the same path not long ago, something like a mentor."
_Keith Lamizana

My name is Keith Lamizana. I am twenty-five years old and the son of the author. To describe myself quickly, I would say I am a curious person who likes to learn and explore opportunities, and this makes me develop an unconventional way of life that has its pros and cons. When I started my studies five years ago, I didn't have any purpose and direction in life.
I was following the conventional path of getting a good diploma, finding a job, and then starting a family.

I have now graduated from my business school, and my life trajectory is not at all what I thought it would be. This is because during these five years I got to travel the world as part of my studies, and this constant exposure to new things and information and multiple personal breakthroughs in my mindset made me realize that in today's world many paths are possible, and some are more urgent than others.

I would define the path I chose as urgent, full of potential, slow, and exciting. This is a path of entrepreneurship where the business I am creating aims to teach people around the world how to build sustainable and regenerative systems (focused mostly on agriculture) to fight against climate change, food and water insecurity, and biodiversity loss.

The path is slow because building a business is a slow process. In doing so, I have to constantly increase my skills and knowledge, which in itself is a life-long journey. In addition, problems like climate change or biodiversity loss are solved across many generations.

The path is full of potential because I make full use of the scalability of the Internet and new digital business models to increase my reach and decouple my time from the creation of value, and ultimately wealth.

The path is exciting because it is part of my vision, which I defined when I was in China. In short, with the current climate crisis, nothing else than working on solutions to this problem made sense, so I decided to go down that road and try to set-up these systems that would create positive externalities as a by-product of their operations.

I went to school in the French system while in Burkina Faso. This context made me take for granted that once I graduated (12th grade), I would move to Europe for my studies. At that time, I did not consider studies in Kenya (where I finished high school) to be a viable course.

It's also good to note that I left two 'nests': the first from Ouagadougou to Nairobi for high school, and the second from Nairobi to France when I left for my studies. I would not change a thing because this path led me to five years of studies where I got the rare opportunity to travel the world, and this opened my eyes to possibilities and changed me in a way I could never have imagined.

Going from Ouagadougou to Nairobi was scary., This was uncharted water, and I was in the middle of puberty with lots of insecurities, so the transition was a big deal.

The language barrier also did not help. But this taught me what it's like to 're-localize' your life somewhere else. Thanks to the first nest living, the second experience was easier. There was still a bit of figuring things out, but I had the chance to have people I could count on, and I was excited about the discoveries I'd make and the freedom I'd taste.

I was excited when I left high school for France. But I struggled with administrative matters and budgeting my money. The areas where I had most trouble were managing my finances and the administrative parts of living alone. That was the big thing for me. Cooking and cleaning were also tricky; I never liked those. The rest was easy. I would usually try to figure things out on my own. When a situation would become critical, I'd ask for help from either my sister or parents. That was usually the last resort.

One recommendation I would like to give is: when you leave your nest to go to a new place, find someone who walked the same path not long ago, something like a mentor. It could be an older sibling, a friend of a sibling, a senior in your high school or university. This person can help you figure things out, and you'll be more comfortable sharing your mistakes with them.

KENNY LAMIZANA, URBAN PLANNER, TWENTY-EIGHT YEARS

Lesson 15: 'Be gentle with yourself on this journey, communicate and seek advice when you feel lost. More importantly, have/rely on your social and emotional support'.
_Kenny Lamizana

I am Kenny Olyvia Gabrielle Yasmin Lamizana. I was born and grew up in Ouagadougou, Burkina Faso. I moved to Canada ten years ago. I first moved to Montreal in 2012 for my undergraduate in urban studies. I then moved to Toronto in 2017 for my master's in urban planning and development. After graduating, I worked for the French school board in Toronto and now work as an urban planner in a

planning and consulting firm. I am a brunch lover who is trying to become a runner, and I keep challenging myself even when terrified. I am continuously learning to get comfortable with discomfort.
Oh—more importantly, home for me is family.

Was I the one who made the choice to leave the nest? Not really, but that was the next step in life—going abroad to study. During your last year in high school, you must: choose a field of study; research undergraduate programs, admissions requirements, and the application process; and apply. Hence, you already know that you will leave at the end of the academic year. You leave because studying abroad is the ultimate means to achieving the best possible higher education (or so we think). Unless Burkina Faso has better universities and higher education institutions, I would do it all over again. But, perhaps I would look for programs closer to home.
Studying abroad comes with a wide range of emotions, mainly when you are over 7,000 kilometers away. At first, I was excited about going abroad, being independent, and living alone, plus I had friends going to Montreal. Then, the time for goodbyes came. That's when it felt real, and it hurt. I remember saying goodbye to my dad first, then dropping my siblings off at high school with my mom, and going home to get ready for the airport.

I won't lie, I cried. I said goodbye to my mom last, and as always, she gave me some advice on navigating life. Still, it would have been easier if I had one of my parents to help me settle in in Montreal like some friends did.

I felt overwhelmed navigating the world alone what with finding accommodation, setting up a bank account, mobile line, and paperwork. I was lucky. I stayed with my childhood friends until moving to a residence;
I could count on my cousin and best friend, who had come a couple months before with their parents and had gone through settling in. It really helped to have a few people, and I wasn't completely alone, although it's different from having your parents.

I thought I was ready and well equipped until I had to open my first bank account, buy furniture, grocery shop, or cook. In a way, parents try to prepare you, but you learn on the job, and they were, after all, just a phone call away. It was probably midnight back home, but I was so lost that I called my dad to ask him how much I should spend on cooking pans and cutlery. I didn't know the cost of living or how much to spend on food or furniture. Learning to navigate the city and use public transit without a smartphone was easier.

My mom always tells me if I can talk and read, I can't get lost, and she is 100% right. As for cooking, I wasn't interested in learning, so I can't blame them for not preparing me.

I would call my parents every time to ask the silliest questions. I also started to listen to musicians/singers my mom used to play back home and burn incense because it comforted me and made me feel close to home. My hometown friends and I would hang out with people from West African countries, whether Niger, Mali, Ivory Coast, Senegal, or Cameroon. Amid homesickness, friendship filled the void.

SARANIA DABEE, URBAN DESIGNER, TWENTY-FOUR

Lesson 16: "You should always never feel embarrassed to ask for help when you are in a foreign country. Always reach out to recruiters or professionals and share your story."
_Sarania Dabee

I am an international student from Mauritius studying architecture and urbanism. I moved to Canada in 2016 and graduated from my program in 2020 with honors and distinction. I am now working for a planning firm as an urban designer.

I made the choice to leave the nest. I wanted to achieve something on my own but also to acquire

experience from abroad as it is valued in Mauritius. I was sad to leave my younger baby sisters, parents, and comfort zone, but thrilled for a new adventure and excited to navigate the world alone.
Did I feel I was ready? Well-equipped with correct tools? Was I confident I got all I needed from my parents for this experience? I never really thought of it at the moment. I remember just trying to take it one day at a time. I always had my parents' support and even today, I have their support in my career choices. I networked a lot during university and built friendships and professional connections to cope with the situation.

BRING IT ALL HOME.

I trust you have enjoyed this journey with me through my own experience and that of wonderful parents and children who kindly agreed to share their amazing lessons. I was thrilled listening to their stories and the life lessons— no matter their age—that they genuinely shared. To make it easier for you to navigate among them and pick the ones that speak to you, I have identified the secrets and lessons below.

THE 7 SECRETS

SECRET #1 *-Acknowledge what is happening, take time to think it through, and make a good decision.*

SECRET #2 *- Adjust and embrace the many other roles you have.*

SECRET #3 *- Take time for fitness and well-being.*

SECRET #4 *- Rediscover your passion and find your life's purpose.*

SECRET #5 *- Socialize, revive, and build your network.*

SECRET #6 - *Dedicate time for stress-free travel.*

SECRET #7 *- Keep contact with your children, and build long-lasting relationships.*

THE 10 LESSONS FOR PARENTS:

LESSON #1: *"Accept that your child is not there to pursue and fulfill your dreams. Make sure you enable your kid to pursue and fulfill its own dreams."*

LESSON #2: *"Be the example. We should raise our children to leave home. It is how nature is.. you don't see male lions staying with the group. He is to go and find his own female."*

LESSON #3: *" Trust the process, release them to fly, walk the path being set for them by allowing God to birth His purpose for our children."*

LESSON #4*:' Give your children the confidence to try things rather than focusing on the risks and the negatives; support their efforts, even if not financially; don't be the one shutting them down, killing their creativity".*

LESSON #5: *" Do your job. Give your children a good foundation You can never give them enough. You can't equip your children with every tool, right"?*

LESSON #6: *" You must stay very close to your children even when they leave the family nest ".*

LESSON #7: *"Be prepared to let your children do their own thing; let them be their own person and Give them the opportunities to experience life on their own".*

LESSON #8: *"As I was a single parent, I wish we could have been two parents because nature has planned it that way and for a reason! ".*

LESSON # 9: *" Keeping communication channels open helps to mature together".*

LESSON #10: *"It's really important to establish and maintain a communication system when the children are small and even when they leave. It's the basis of everything. And then being present, and listening."*

THE 6 LESSONS FOR CHILDREN:

LESSON #1: *"To any kid leaving to go abroad, I would say, when you move to a new country, be open to learning and discovering."*

LESSON #2: *"Focus on why you left your comfort zone and your parent's nest, and do not derail from your goal!"*

LESSON #3: *"Ask questions; don't buckle up on things that you can get advice on. Always try to find someone, a reliable source to seek guidance."*

LESSON #4: *"When you live your nest to go in a new place, find someone who walked the same path not long ago, something like a mentor.""*

LESSON #5: *"Be gentle with yourself on this journey. Communicate and seek advice when you feel lost. More importantly, have/rely on your social and emotional support."*

LESSON #6: *"You should never feel embarrassed to ask for help when you are in a foreign country."*

I would also love to hear your story and your life lessons. Please reach out if you wish to share. I do hope that you have taken time to reflect using the instant action space provided all along. The space was meant to help you.

Indeed, while reading the different experiences and coping mechanisms, you can take these pieces of advice and use them to transform or improve some habits and areas in your life. Only by taking action, can you reap the benefits and live a healthy, happier, and fulfilled life.

ONE LAST MESSAGE

Congratulations

I am so proud of you for making the great decision to read this book all the way to the end. I hope you have enjoyed this journey with me and found the coping mechanisms and personal stories in this book though provoking and useful.

Things constantly change in our lives, and hence, the need to cultivate the ability to truly accept whatever comes and embrace it. My mission with this book was to serve you and make a positive difference in your life by inspiring you to embrace whatever life throws your way; to look at the challenges that come with changes and turn them into stepping stones for a more fulfilled life.

I learnt so much through the conversation I had with the amazing parents and grown children who agreed to share their experiences and lessons learned. These lessons are priceless for parents still facing the challenges of being empty nesters or who are yet to become empty nesters.

My hope is that you have been both inspired and empowered—to DO more, BE more, and ACHIEVE more—than you ever thought possible.

Now that you've read the book, you can always revisit it and pick one more secret to add to your life improvement routine. Share this book with someone you care about.

ACKNOWLEDGEMENTS

Through the years, many people have blessed me with their ideas, mentoring, and support, each impacting my life in a different, meaningful way. I am deeply indebted to Ibrahim Thiaw, who shaped my professional life by his mentorship, guidance and tough leadership: Merci.

To thank everyone is impossible, and I apologize for anyone not listed. Please know that I appreciate you greatly. In no particular order, I am hugely grateful to:

my special 'wingmen' Kolene, Kenny, and Keith Lamizana for your unfailingly honest feedback, keen insight and unwavering support;

with special thanks to the amazing parents: Amanda Khozi Mukwashi, Lydia Eibl-Kamolleh, Christopher and Tanya Cox, Safia Barry, Celina Ray, Vincent Sweeney, Sandy Lowe, Christine James, Gisela Maria Mahler, Abdoulaye and Hulda Diallo;

and children (or should I say young adults?): Aurélie Chapon, Faiza Congo, Sarania Dabee, Kenny Lamizana, Keith Lamizana, and Kolene Lamizana for taking time to share their experiences. I am so grateful;

Joanne Marie Clark, for taking time to review, edit my book, and also share a special gift with me.
Your suggestions brought undeniable added value to the book;
Jeanne Mason, for editing this book;
James Malinchaks, Nick and Megan Unsworth, to whom I am so grateful for all the training, tips and encouragement that gave me the courage and the tools to take my message to the world;
to the people we meet along the way who bring their unique skills and free us from doing things for which we have no natural talent —a huge thanks to all the support system network who gave me their testimonials;
to my cheering and uplifting group: Mohamed Kara, Wendy Yawkins, Christine James, Dr. Ukpong Nwankwo. You kept me going and were always there for me. Thank you!
and the last shall be first:
to my family, without whom I couldn't have become the person I am.
Thank you from the bottom of my heart.

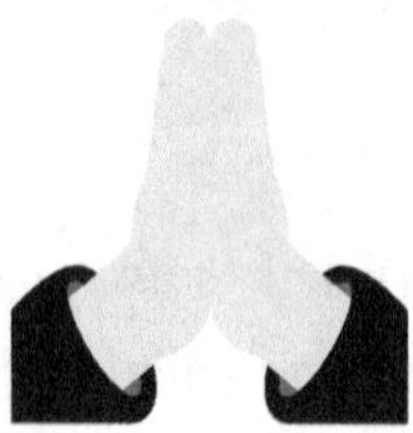

FREE

Special Free Bonus Gift For You

To help you reach your potential, there *are* **FREE BONUS RESOURCES** FOR **YOU** at:

www.emptynestfulloflife.com

about

BIRGUY

Birguy Lamizana Diallo is an astute professional whose work is grounded in solving real-world issues relating to water, wastewater, wetland conservation, land restoration and human-environmental interactions.

She participated in the Steering Committee of IUCN CEM and has represented Africa for many years. She is currently recognized as an Emeritus CEM member.

In her capacity as a fellow of the international Visitor Programme of the US Department of State, a grantee of the International Foundation for Sciences (IFS) and a Melvin John Companion in the Lions Club International, Birguy epitomises the admirable attributes of a modern, educated role model and inspiring visionary ahead of her time with her exceptional knowledge and intelligence.

Currently, Birguy works for the UN to support countries in the Emblematic Africa Great Green Wall.

Birguy and her husband raised three children: two girls and a boy. Once her children left the nest, she experienced and dealt with the empty nest firsthand.

Birguy

Printed in Great Britain
by Amazon

38756394R00119